Chapter 1: Addition 1

Adding – pairs that make 10

Cut out a piece of squared paper,
10 squares by 10 squares, and colour it like this:

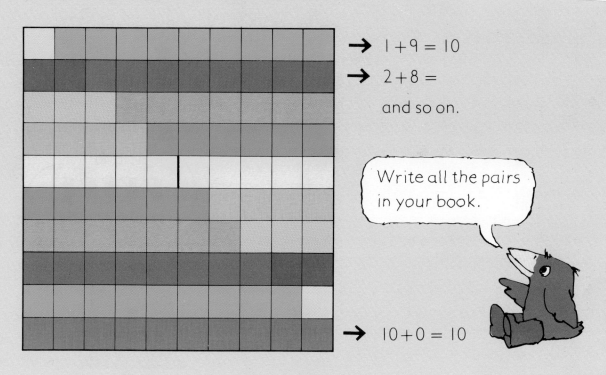

→ $1 + 9 = 10$

→ $2 + 8 =$

and so on.

Write all the pairs in your book.

→ $10 + 0 = 10$

The tens race

Choose a race.

Copy the column of figures.

What must be added to each figure to make 10?

Race against your partner or the clock.

Race 1	Race 2	Race 3	Race 4
7 + 3	4	5	3
2 + 8	8	9	1
5 + 5	1	4	9
6	5	7	2
9	6	2	5
4	7	3	7
8	2	6	8
3	9	8	6
1	3	1	4

WINNING POST

Making an addition square

Take a piece of squared paper, 12 squares by 12 squares,
and make an addition square like this:

+	0	1	2	3	4	5	6	7	8	9	10
10											
9											
8											
7			10								
6											
5											
4											
3											
2											
1											
0											

Remember:

Columns go up and down

and

rows go across.

The addition square is filled in like this:

+	0	1	2	3
7				10
6				
5				
4				
3				
2				
1				
0				

The ⌐ shape shows the square where
the 3 column and 7 row cross.

10 is put in this square
because $3 + 7 = 10$.

Fill in all the answers on
your addition square.

1 Find these patterns in your square:
a 5, 5, 5, 5, 5, 5.
b 1, 3, 5, 7, 9, 11, 13, 15, 17, 19.
c 10,10,10,10,10,10,10,10,10,10,10.

This domino is called a "double six" and counts $6+6 = 12$.

1 Copy and complete these doubles.

a $2+2 =$ **e** $3+3 =$ **i** $4+4 =$

b $5+5 =$ **f** $6+6 =$ **j** $7+7 =$

c $8+8 =$ **g** $9+9 =$ **k** $10+10 =$

d $0+0 =$ **h** $1+1 =$

All these "doubles" are in one sloping line on your addition square. Shade them in so that you can see the pattern.

2 All the answers to these are more than 10 and less than 20. Use your addition square. Copy and complete.

Block A

$7+5 =$

$9+5 =$

$6+5 =$

$8+5 =$

Block B

$8+6 =$

$5+6 =$

$9+6 =$

$7+6 =$

$6+6 =$

Block C

$6+7 =$

$9+7 =$

$4+7 =$

$8+7 =$

$5+7 =$

$7+7 =$

Block D

$5+8 =$

$7+8 =$

$3+8 =$

$9+8 =$

$6+8 =$

$4+8 =$

$8+8 =$

Block E

$6+9 =$

$5+9 =$

$8+9 =$

$4+9 =$

$3+9 =$

$7+9 =$

$6+9 =$

Block F

$9 + \boxed{} = 11$

$\boxed{} + 3 = 11$

$7 + \boxed{} = 11$

$\boxed{} + 5 = 11$

Block G

$\boxed{} + 3 = 12$

$8 + \boxed{} = 12$

$7 + \boxed{} = 12$

$\boxed{} + 6 = 12$

Block H

$9 + \boxed{} = 13$

$\boxed{} + 5 = 13$

$7 + \boxed{} = 13$

$\boxed{} + 6 = 15$

$8 + \boxed{} = 15$

$9 + \boxed{} = 17$

Block I

$\boxed{} + 5 = 14$

$8 + \boxed{} = 14$

$\boxed{} + 7 = 14$

$9 + \boxed{} = 16$

$\boxed{} + 8 = 16$

$\boxed{} + 9 = 18$

A useful discovery

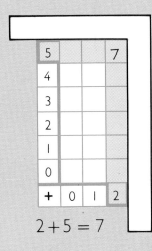

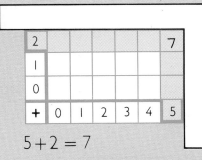

All you do is turn the L shape over.

2+5 = 7

5+2 = 7

We can write this
as:
2+5 = 7 = 5+2

I Copy and complete:

a 6+3= 9 = 3+☐   **e** 7+☐ = 9 = 2+7   **i** 10+☐=18=☐+10

b 8+4=12 = 4+☐   **f** 6+5 =☐ = 5+6   **j** ☐ +6 = 15 = 6+☐

c 7+8=15 =☐+7   **g** 9+7 =☐ = 7+9   **k** 9+☐ = 17 =☐ +9

d ☐ +8 =17= 8+9   **h** 7+☐ = 12 =☐ +7   **l** 8+6 =☐ = 6+8

The order in which
we add two numbers
does not alter the total.
We can show this
by using rods.

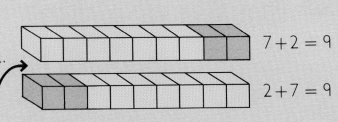

7+2 = 9

2+7 = 9

We can show it on the number line too:

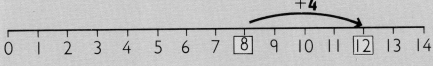

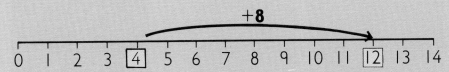

Start at 8 and count on 4 }
Start at 4 and count on 8 } → 12   8+4 = 12 = 4+8

Use a strip of squared paper to make a number line from 0 to 20.

1   Use colours to show that:

   a $8+4 = 4+8$ **b** $9+5 = 5+9$ **c** $3+10 = 10+3$ **d** $6+11 = 11+6$

How can this discovery be useful?
If you know $12+7 = 19$, then you also know $7+12 = 19$.

2   Use these: to answer these:

$9+ 4 = 13$	**a** $12+18 = \Box$
$18+12 = 30$	**b** $26+24 = \Box$
$24+32 = 56$	**c** $4+ 9 = \Box$
$17+12 = 29$	**d** $11+29 = \Box$
$24+26 = 50$	**e** $12+17 = \Box$
$29+11 = 40$	**f** $32+24 = \Box$

It is easier to start at 14 and count on 3 to answer $14+ 3 = \Box$
than it is to start at 3 and count on 14 to answer $3+14 = \Box$

This is easier:

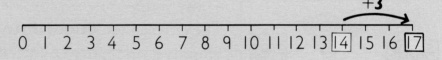

than this:

3 Copy these into your book and use the easier way to find the answers:

   a $4+9 = 9+ 4 =$ **d** $15+ 0 = 0+15 =$ **g** $5+14 = 14+5 =$

   b $17+1 = 1+17 =$ **e** $2+13 = 13+ 2 =$ **h** $6+12 = 12+6 =$

   c $11+5 = 5+11 =$ **f** $17+ 3 = 3+17 =$ **i** $4+16 = 16+4 =$

Chapter 2: Shape 1

Sorting shapes

This shape has **straight** sides.

This shape has **curved** sides.

This shape has both **straight** and **curved** sides.

I Look at these shapes.

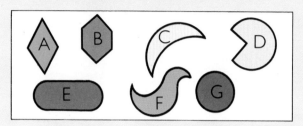

List the letters of the shapes with:
a straight sides only,
b curved sides only,
c straight and curved sides.

2 Draw 4 shapes with:
a straight sides only, **b** curved sides only,
c both straight and curved sides.

Shapes with 3 or more sides

These shapes have 3 sides and 3 corners.
They are called **triangles**.

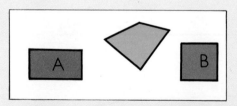

These shapes have 4 sides and 4 corners.
They are called **quadrilaterals**.
Shapes A and B are called **rectangles**.
Shape A is an oblong. Shape B is a square.

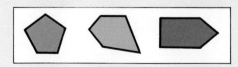

These shapes have 5 sides and 5 corners.
They are called **pentagons**.

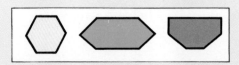

These shapes have 6 sides and 6 corners.
They are called **hexagons**.

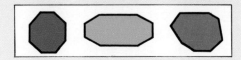

These shapes have 8 sides and 8 corners.
They are called **octagons**.

I Look at these shapes.

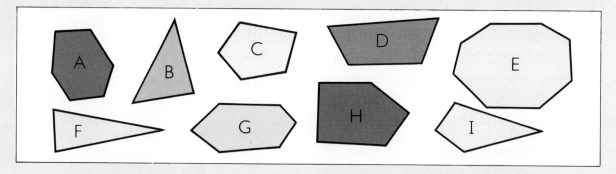

Write a sentence about each shape.

The first one is done for you : Shape A is a hexagon.

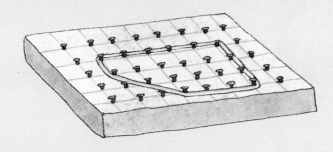

This shape has been made by stretching an elastic band over nails on a nailboard.

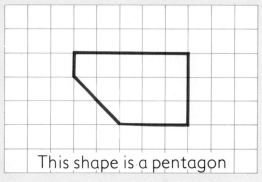

This shape is a pentagon

This shape has been recorded on squared paper.

2 Make these shapes on a nailboard.
Draw them on squared paper.

  a 4 different shaped triangles.

  b 4 different shaped quadrilaterals.

  c 4 different shaped pentagons.

  d 4 different shaped hexagons.

  e 4 different shaped octagons.

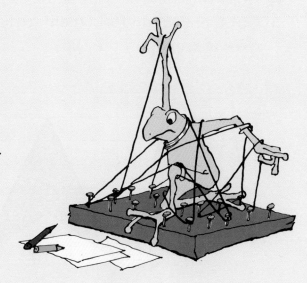

Axes of symmetry

Copy this quadrilateral onto squared paper and then cut it out.

Fold the shape so that one part fits **exactly onto the other**

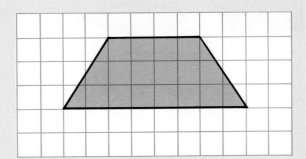 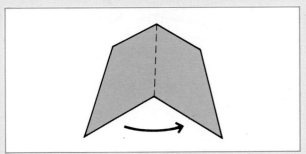

The fold is an **axis of symmetry**

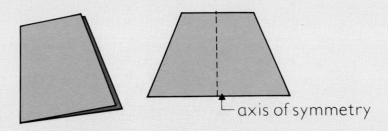

axis of symmetry

Some shapes have more than one axis of symmetry.

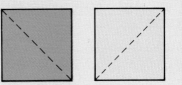

A square has 4 axes of symmetry.

I Copy these shapes onto squared paper.
Cut them out and fold them to discover how many
axes of symmetry they have.

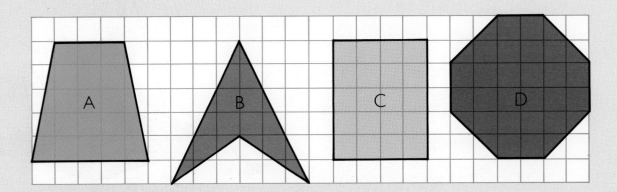

These figures have
axes of symmetry.

If we fold them up
their middles, one half
would fit exactly
on the other.

These advertisements
have axes of
symmetry.

1 Collect some examples of symmetry from newspapers and magazines.
Stick them in your book.
Write a sentence for each shape.

2 In the picture, only half of each shape is drawn.
The dotted line is an axis of symmetry.
Copy them onto squared paper and complete the shapes.
The first one is done for you.

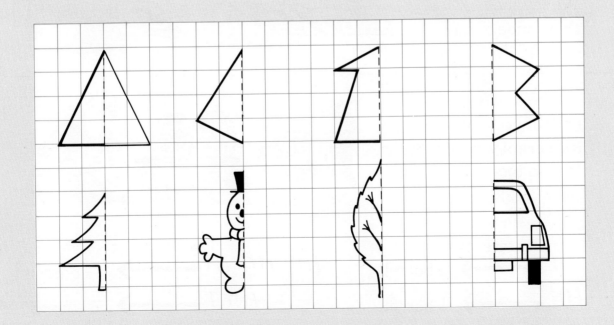

Chapter 3: Place value

Tallying

Many years ago, people knew nothing about
the numbers we use today.
How do you think this man was able to tell his friend on
the other side of the river how many weapons he had?

Who had more weapons?

Sometimes they made
knots along a piece
of string, or made
patterns with stones
or shells.
We say that
they made a tally.

Early merchants used
a different way of tallying
to help them count
their goods.

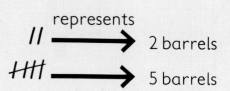

represents

|| ⟶ 2 barrels

||||| ⟶ 5 barrels

||||| ||||| ||| ⟶ 13 barrels

||||| | ⟶ 6 barrels

1 Copy and fill in how many barrels have been counted.

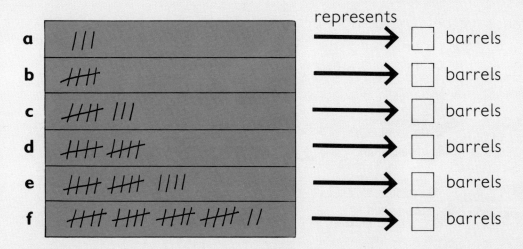

represents

a ||| → ☐ barrels

b 卌 → ☐ barrels

c 卌 ||| → ☐ barrels

d 卌 卌 → ☐ barrels

e 卌 卌 |||| → ☐ barrels

f 卌 卌 卌 卌 || → ☐ barrels

g Why does it help to know your 5 times table?

2 Record using columns.
Copy and complete.

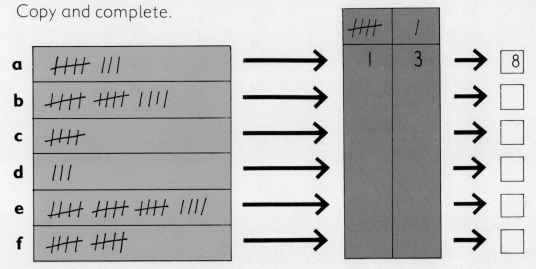

a 卌 ||| → | 卌 | / | → ☐
                 | 1 | 3 | → 8

b 卌 卌 |||| → ☐

c 卌 → ☐

d ||| → ☐

e 卌 卌 卌 |||| → ☐

f 卌 卌 → ☐

A traffic survey

3 Count the number of vehicles passing your school in 15 minutes.
It is easier if different children look for different vehicles.
For example:

Simon	Mary	Jane
cars buses	vans lorries	bicycles motor bikes

Understanding place value

At Mr Sweet's factory, 5 choc-bars are packed into a box. If he had 8 bars he would say, "I have one full box and three bars," and he would record: →

boxes	units
1	3

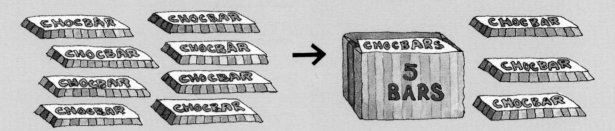

1 Copy and complete.

number of bars		boxes	units
a	9		
b	12		
c	15		
d	17		
e	23		

2 Copy and complete.

	boxes	units	number of bars
a	1	2	
b	0	3	
c	1	4	
d	2	4	
e	3	3	

Mrs Giles packs eggs in boxes.
Each box holds 6 eggs.
She keeps a record of eggs sold each day.

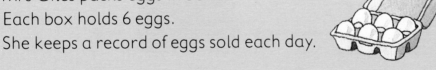

3 Copy and complete.

	eggs sold		boxes	eggs
Mon.	9	→	1	3
Tues.	11	→		
Wed.	12	→		
Thur.	16	→		
Fri.	18	→		
Sat.	5	→		
Sun.	13	→		

4 Copy and complete.

days		weeks	days
8	→	1	1
10	→		
6	→		
7	→		
14	→		
23	→		
18	→		
30	→		

Grouping in threes

3 units make a long.
3 longs make a square.

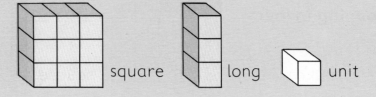

square · long · unit

Every time you have 3 units, exchange them for I long.

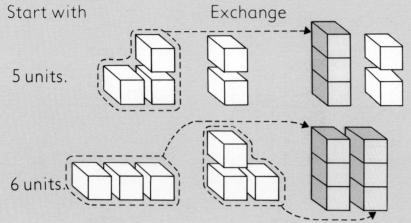

Start with · Exchange

5 units.

6 units.

Record as :

longs	units
1	2
2	0

I Use units and longs. Copy and complete.

	longs	units
4 units		
7 units		

	longs	units
3 units		
8 units		

Every time you have 3 longs, exchange them for I square.
Start with II units.

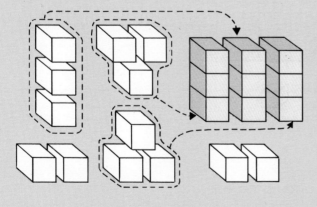
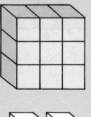

Record as:

squares	longs	units
1	0	2

2 Using units, longs and squares,
group these units in threes:
10 units, 12 units, 14 units, 9 units,
15 units, 17 units, 20 units, and
22 units. The first is done for you:

	squares	longs	units
10 units	1	0	1

Grouping in fours

4 units make a long.
4 longs make a square.

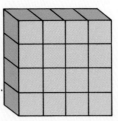 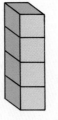 square   long unit

Every time you have 4 units, exchange them for 1 long.

Start with   Exchange   Record as:

7 units.

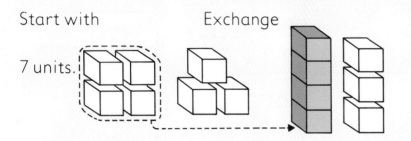

longs	units
1	3

1   Use units and longs. Copy and complete.

	longs	units
6 units		
8 units		

	longs	units
11 units		
12 units		

Every time you have 4 longs, exchange them for 1 square.

Start with 17 units.   Exchange   Record as:

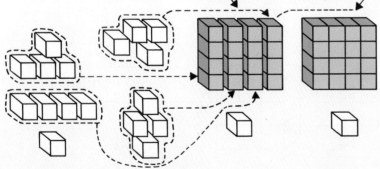

squares	longs	units
1	0	1

2   Use units, longs and squares. Copy and complete.

	squares	longs	units
18 units			
16 units			
19 units			

	squares	longs	units
20 units			
21 units			
24 units			

Grouping in tens

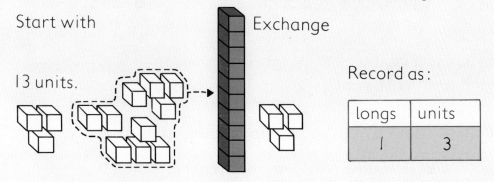

10 units make a long.
10 longs make a square.

square   long   unit

Every time you have 10 units, change them for 1 long.

Start with   Exchange

13 units.

→

Record as:

longs	units
1	3

Grouping in tens is used for our everyday numbers.

2 tens and 3 units → 20 + 3 = 23

I Use longs (tens) and units to set out these. Copy and complete.

1 ten and 3 units	10 + 3		thirteen
1 ten and 7 units		17	
1 ten and 9 units	10 + 9		nineteen
	10 + 6		sixteen
2 tens and 0 units	20 + 0		
2 tens and 5 units			twenty-five
	20 + 8		twenty-eight
3 tens and 1 unit		31	
6 tens and 0 units		60	
9 tens and 3 units			
4 tens and 4 units			forty-four

Chapter 4: Length 1

Measuring with parts of your body

You can use these parts
of your body
to measure objects
in your classroom.

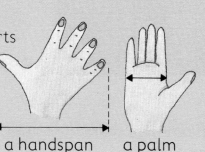

a handspan   a palm

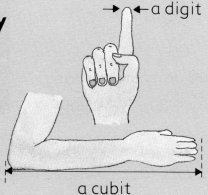

a digit

a cubit

1 Why would you use a digit
to measure the length of a pencil?

2 Which part of your body would you use to measure these:

a a book?   **c** your desk?   **e** your teacher's desk?

b the door?   **d** a paintbrush?   **f** a cupboard

Record like this: **a** I would use my palm to measure a book.

Estimating before measuring

Bill thinks, "My finger will fit
8 times along my pencil."
He estimates that his finger will fit 8 times.

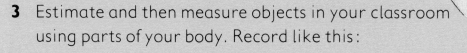

But when he uses his finger to measure with
he finds that the pencil is 9 finger widths.

3 Estimate and then measure objects in your classroom
using parts of your body. Record like this:

object	body measure used	estimate	actual measurement
pencil	digits	8	9

Measuring longer distances

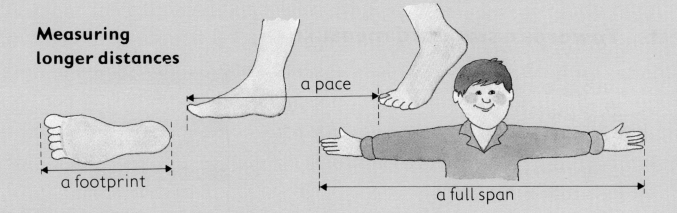

a pace

a footprint

a full span

1 To measure these distances, use one of the body measures.
Estimate first, then measure. Record like this:

distance	measure used	estimate	actual measurement
Length of classroom			
Width of classroom			
Length of display board			
Teacher's desk to the door			
Length of playground			
Width of window			

The bits left over

Sometimes when we measure with a part of our body,
there is a bit left over.
We have to use a smaller measure for this.
John measured the width of this desk.
It measured 3 spans and a bit left over.
He measured this in digits.

He recorded:
The width of the desk is 3 spans and 2 digits.

2 Use two parts of your body to measure these
and record your findings in your book.

  a The width of your classroom door.
  b The length of the blackboard.
  c The width of your desk.
  d The length of your classroom.

Towards a standard measure

Cut a strip of coloured
sticky paper to
the length of your span

Compare it with
the length of the strips
of four other children.

Are they all the same?

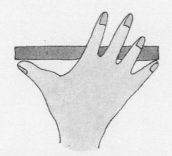

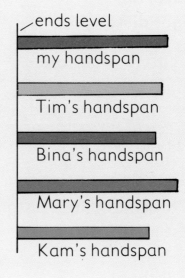

ends level

my handspan

Tim's handspan

Bina's handspan

Mary's handspan

Kam's handspan

The metre

All metre sticks are the same length.
A metre is a **standard unit**.

I   Make lists of objects which are:

shorter than one metre	about one metre	longer than one metre
width of door	my desk	window

Estimate first then use your metre stick to measure.
Record like this – use m to stand for metre or metres.

	estimate	measurement
length of blackboard	2m	3m
height of door		
width of classroom		
length of corridor		
distance of my desk from door		

The 10 centimetre (decimetre) rod

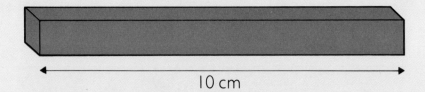

10 cm

This is a decimetre rod. It is 10 centimetres long.
We write cm to stand for centimetre or centimetres.

1 How many times will it fit along your metre stick?
   Record like this:
   My decimetre rod fits ☐ times along my metre stick.

2 Use your 10 cm rods
   to measure objects which
   are shorter than 1 metre.
   Estimate before measuring.

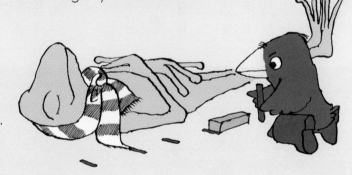

   Record like this:

object	estimate	measurement
my reading book	1 decimetre rod	2 decimetre rods

Sometimes when we use the metre stick to measure an object,
there is a bit left over. We can use the 10 centimetre rod
to measure this bit.

3 Use your metre stick and 10 centimetre rod to measure 10 things.
   Record like this:

	estimate		measurement	
	whole m	10 cm rods	whole m	10 cm rods
length of teacher's desk	1	5	1	6

Chapter 5: Addition 2

Counting on from 10, 20, etc.

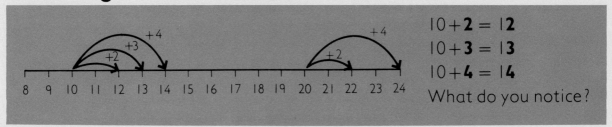

$10+\mathbf{2} = 12$
$10+\mathbf{3} = 13$
$10+\mathbf{4} = 14$

What do you notice?

1 Copy into your book and complete:

a $10+ 5 =$ **e** $20+2 =$ **i** $30+ 3 =$ **m** $40+2 =$
b $10+ 6 =$ **f** $20+4 =$ **j** $30+ 6 =$ **n** $40+6 =$
c $10+ 8 =$ **g** $20+7 =$ **k** $30+ 8 =$ **o** $50+7 =$
d $10+10 =$ **h** $20+9 =$ **l** $30+10 =$ **p** $60+4 =$

Look at
these
three
additions:

$$4 + 3 + 7$$
$$7 + 7$$
$$14$$

$$4 + 3 + 7$$
$$4 + 10$$
$$14$$

$$4 + 3 + 7$$
$$11 + 3$$
$$14$$

Does it matter which order we use to add the numbers?

$$3 + 6 + 7 + 4 + 2$$
$$10 \quad 10 + 2 = 22$$

By spotting pairs of numbers which make 10, the addition is easier and quicker.

2 Estimate first by spotting tens, then complete.

a $4+8+6+2+3 =$ **c** $9+7+1+3+5 =$ **e** $6+5+4+5+1 =$
b $3+7+9+5+5 =$ **d** $8+7+5+3+2 =$ **f** $9+2+1+8+4 =$

3 Write the answer only to the following:

a $5+3+0+5 =$ **d** $2+8+8+2 =$ **g** $3+8+2+4+7 =$
b $4+2+6+1 =$ **e** $9+9+1+1 =$ **h** $6+4+9+3 =$
c $3+7+4+6 =$ **f** $3+1+7+9 =$ **i** $10+3+4+6 =$

Make up some more of your own.

Patterns in addition

If
a number strip
is cut into
10 slices
10 units long,
it makes
a 100 square
and can
be used for
adding.

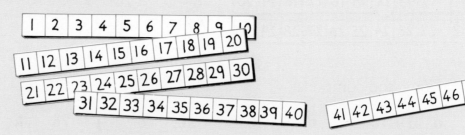

Start at 2.
Count on 3 hops.
Finish at 5.

$2 + 3 = 5$

Look for a pattern
to help you estimate.

1 Use a copy of the 100 square to answer these:

a $3+6=$	**e** $8+4=$	**i** $7+9=$	**m** $24+10=$
b $13+6=$	**f** $28+4=$	**j** $17+9=$	**n** $24+12=$
c $23+6=$	**g** $48+4=$	**k** $27+9=$	**o** $54+10=$
d $53+6=$	**h** $68+4=$	**l** $37+9=$	**p** $54+12=$

Make up some more of your own.

2 Use your own 100 square. Copy and fill in the missing numbers.

a Count on in fives from 2 to 32: 2, 7, 12, ☐, ☐, ☐, 32.

b Count on in sevens from 4 to 39: 4, 11, ☐, ☐, ☐, 39.

c 14, 16, 18, 20, ☐, ☐, ☐.   **f** 1, 4, 7, 10, ☐, ☐, ☐.

d 10, 20, 30, 40, ☐, ☐, ☐.   **g** 7, 17, 27, 37, ☐, ☐, ☐.

e 5, 10, 15, 20, ☐, ☐, ☐.   **h** 10, 19, 28, 37, ☐, ☐, ☐.

1	2	3	④	5	6	7	8	9	10
11	12	13	⑭	15	16	17	18	19	20
21	22	23	24	25	26	27	28	29	30

4 + 10 = 14
18 + 10 = 28
Why is it easy to count on 10
on a 100 square?

1 Copy and complete.

a 13 + 10 =   **e** 6 + 10 =

b 23 + 10 =   **f** 36 + 10 =

c 13 + 20 =   **g** 16 + 20 =

d 13 + 30 =   **h** 16 + 30 =

i	8	**j**	28	**k**	48	**l**	18
	+10		+10		+10		+20
	___		___		___		___

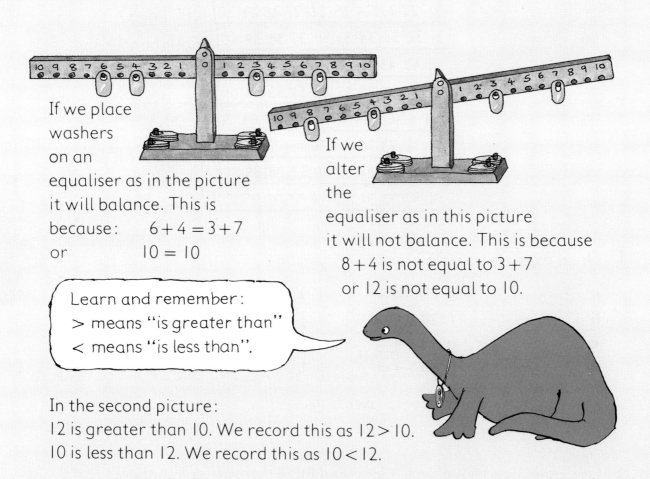

If we place
washers
on an
equaliser as in the picture
it will balance. This is
because: 6 + 4 = 3 + 7
or   10 = 10

If we
alter
the
equaliser as in this picture
it will not balance. This is because
   8 + 4 is not equal to 3 + 7
   or 12 is not equal to 10.

Learn and remember:
> means "is greater than"
< means "is less than".

In the second picture:
12 is greater than 10. We record this as 12 > 10.
10 is less than 12. We record this as 10 < 12.

2 Write the number sentences with their correct signs: = , > or < .

a 8 + 7 ☐ 7 + 8

b 6 + 7 ☐ 6 + 6

c 6 + 7 ☐ 6 + 8

d 9 + 2 ☐ 8 + 3

e 5 + 5 + 4 ☐ 8 + 2 + 2

f 1 + 0 + 2 + 8 ☐ 1 + 0 + 2 + 9

g 8 + 7 + 3 ☐ 4 + 9 + 4

h 10 + 7 ☐ 9 + 8 + 1

Magic squares

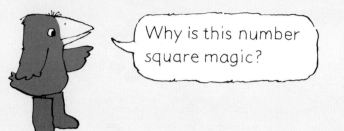

Why is this number square magic?

	8	1	6
A→	8	1	6
B→	3	5	7
C→	4	9	2

G↗ ↑ ↑ ↑ ↖H

D E F

The numbers
in row **A** |8|1|6|
added together:
8 + 1 + 6 = 15

Add the numbers
in row **B**.

Add the numbers
in row **C**.

These are
the numbers
in column **D**
 8
 3
 4
added together:
8 + 3 + 4 = 15

Add the numbers
in column **E**.

Add the numbers
in column **F**.

These are
the numbers in
diagonal **G**
 6
 5
 4
add together:
4 + 5 + 6 = 15

Add the numbers
in diagonal **H**.

I Is this
a Magic
Square?

7	8	3
2	6	10
9	4	5

Each small
square is
called
a cell.

←a cell

2 Here are some
Magic Squares
with some empty
cells.
Copy them
and work out
the missing
numbers.

a
	9	2
		7
	1	6

b
9		7
4		
5		

c
10		8
	7	
		4

d
2		
6	1	8

e
3		
7	2	9

f
5	12	
		8
		11

The computer
The pointers
on the computer
say **+ 3**
so it will add 3
to each numeral
fed into the machine.

The computer records all the inputs and outputs
on a print-out-tape.

+ 3	Input	20	10	0	8	5	2	24	14	4
	Output	23	13	3	11	8	5	27	17	7

Check the tape to see if
the computer is working properly.

Look for patterns to help you estimate.
Copy and complete these tapes:

1

+ 6	Input	9	19	29	39	49	0	6	12	18	24
	Output	15					6				

2

+ 10	Input	0	10	30	50	60	3	13	53	23	33
	Output										

3

+ 9	Input	5	7	8	11	21	31	0	9	18	27
	Output										

Make up some more tapes of your own.

Chapter 6: Money 1

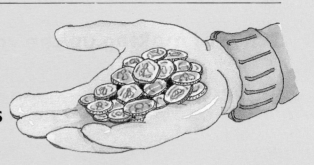

Looking closely at our coins

Get out some school money or some real money and carefully place each coin on top of its picture.

I Write in your book which coins have these pictures:

a	**b**	**c**	**d**	**e**	**f**
Britannia	The Thistle of Scotland	3 ostrich feathers	Rose and Crown	A portcullis	The Lion of England

'p' stands for penny.
If we have more than
one penny, we say pence.

 one penny   two pence  ten pence

Sorting coins

2 Take a handful of coins.
Sort them into
piles of the same value.

Write in your book :

a I have ☐ 20p coins.   **c** I have ☐ 10p coins.   **e** I have ☐ 5p coins.

b I have ☐ 2p coins.   **d** I have ☐ 1p coins.   **f** I have ☐ 50p coins.

Ask someone to check this for you.

Ways of making up the value of a coin

The 5p coin This is the smallest 'silver' coin. We can exchange it for 'bronze' coins like this:

 and  and the same value as

To record this in your book draw round the coins and write their values in the circles like this:

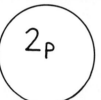 and 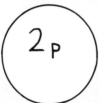 and are worth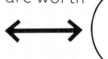

1 Find 2 more ways of making up 5p.

The 10p coin

 The 10p coin has the same value as:

two 5p coins

or five 2p coins

or ten 1p coins

2 Find 5 more ways of making 10p. Record these in your book.

The 20p coin

 The 20p coin has the same value as:

two 10p coins

or
four 5p coins

or
ten 2p coins

or
twenty 1p coins

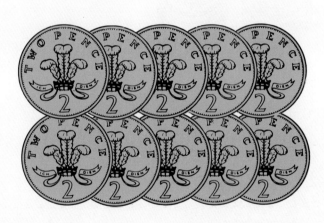

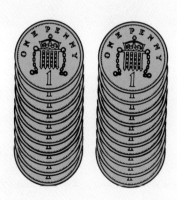

I Find 5 more ways of making up 20p. Record like this:

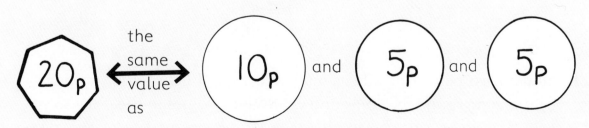

The 50p coin

Here is the 50p coin.
It has
the same value as:

or

five 10p coins

ten 5p coins

or
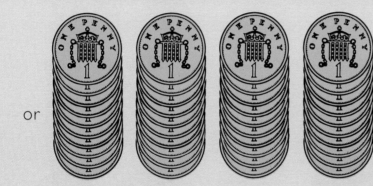
fifty 1p coins.

We can have a mixture of coins equal in value to 50p:

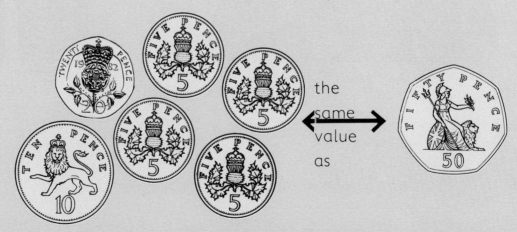

the
same
value
as

1 Find 5 ways of making 50p using mixed coins. Record your answers
by drawing round the coins and write their values in the circles.

Using coins to make amounts

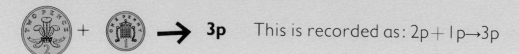 + → **3p**   This is recorded as: 2p+1p→3p

1 Do these recording them in your book in the same way.

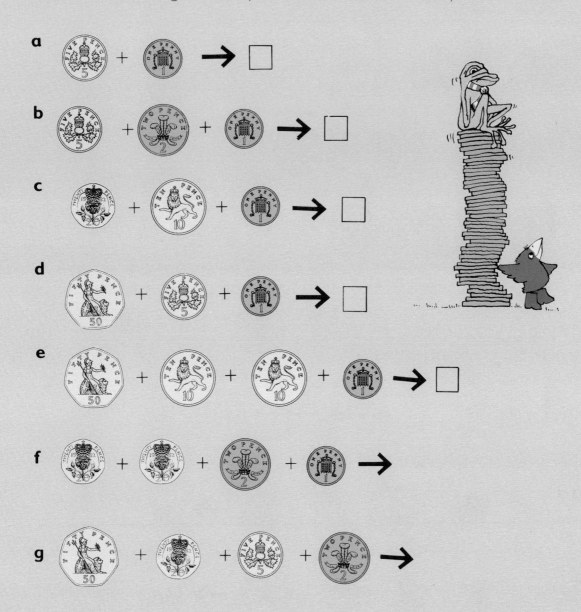

a ⬜

b ⬜

c ⬜

d ⬜

e ⬜

f →

g →

2 Find 3 ways of making each of these amounts. Use your coins.
Draw round them and record their values in the circles.

a 6p	**c** 12p	**e** 9p	**g** 57p	**i** 41p	**k** 35p
b 10p	**d** 15p	**f** 70p	**h** 20p	**j** 31p	**l** 87p

Finding the missing coin

1 Susan and her 3 friends should have 10p each but they each have one coin missing. Write in your book which coin is missing.

a

b

c

d

2 The coins you can see are worth 8p, the total is 10p, so the missing coin is 2p.

    10p

Record like this: 8p + 2p ⟶ 10p

Record these in the same way:

a   → 9p

b → 44p

c → 68p

d → 47p

Giving change by counting on

You go into the shop to buy a toffee apple.

The price is You give the shopkeeper

He starts at the price and counts out
the change till he reaches the money you gave him:

Seven pence . . .   and I makes 8 . . .   and 2 makes 10.

The total change is **3p**.

I Use coins to count out the change for these.
In your book draw round the coins and write down the total change.

	Price	Coins given to shopkeeper		Price	Coins given to shopkeeper
a	4p	TEN PENCE 10	**e**	11p	10p 5p
b	8p	10p	**f**	14p	10p 10p
c	5p	2p 2p 2p	**g**	21p	10p 10p 5p
d	40p	50p	**h**	38p	50p

Chapter 7: Subtraction 1

Finding the difference

Lynne and Karen are Brownies.

Lynne has
6 badges:

Karen has
4 badges:

Lynne has 2 more badges than Karen. Karen has 2 less badges than Lynne.
(Some people say "2 fewer than".)

The difference between 6 and 4 is 2:   6 − 4 = 2.

If Karen gets 2 more badges, she will have the same number as Lynne
because 4 + 2 = 6.

Copy and complete these number sentences.
Use cubes or squared paper if you need them.

1   **a** 7 − 3 = ☐   **b** 3 + ☐ = 7

2 a 8 − 2 = ☐   **4 a** 9 + ☐ = 14   **6 a** 19 − 13 = ☐   **8 a** 20 − 14 = ☐

b 2 + ☐ = 8   **b** 14 − 9 = ☐   **b** ☐ − 6 = 13   **b** ☐ + 14 = 20

c 8 − 6 = ☐   **c** 5 + ☐ = 14   **c** ☐ + 6 = 19   **c** 6 + ☐ = 20

d 6 + ☐ = 8   **d** 14 − 5 = ☐   **d** 13 + ☐ = 19   **d** ☐ = 20 − 6

3 a 12 − 7 = ☐   **5 a** 16 − 9 = ☐   **7 a** 8 + ☐ = 15   **9 a** 18 − 9 = ☐

b 12 − ☐ = 5   **b** 9 + ☐ = 16   **b** ☐ + 7 = 15   **b** ☐ + 6 = 14

c 7 + ☐ = 12   **c** 7 + ☐ = 16   **c** ☐ − 7 = 8   **c** 12 + ☐ = 17

d 5 + ☐ = 12   **d** 16 − 7 = ☐   **d** ☐ = 15 − 8   **d** ☐ = 16 − 8

There are lots of things we can say or write about this diagram:

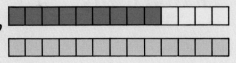

What we **say** in words.	What we **write** in a number sentence.
9 and 4 make 13.	$9 + 4 = 13$
9 plus 4 equals 13.	$9 + 4 = 13$
The difference between 13 and 9 is 4.	$13 - 9 = 4$
13 is 4 more than 9.	$13 = 9 + 4$
9 is 4 less than 13.	$9 = 13 - 4$
The difference between 13 and 4 is 9.	$13 - 4 = 9$
9 less than 13 is 4.	$13 - 9 = 4$

Write down as many number sentences as you can about this diagram:

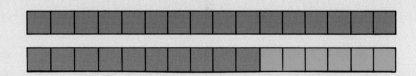

These letters are called vowels:

a e i o u

John chose five lines from his reading book and kept a tally to count the number of times each vowel was used. Then he made a graph on squared paper to show his results clearly.

a	⊬⊬ ⊬⊬ IIII	14
e	⊬⊬ ⊬⊬ ⊬⊬ ⊬⊬	20
i	⊬⊬ III	8
o	⊬⊬ ⊬⊬ I	11
u	⊬⊬ II	7

John's tally

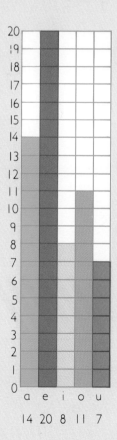

14 20 8 11 7

There are 6 more e's than a's. $20 = 14 + 6$
The difference between the number of o's and the number of u's is 4. $11 - 7 = 4$.

1 a Write some more number sentences about John's graph.

  b Choose some lines from your reading book and make a tally of the number of vowels.

  c Draw a graph and compare it with John's graph. Write some number sentences about your graph.

Taking away

In the last section we used subtraction to find the **difference**
between two numbers. We also subtract to find how many objects
are left after some have been removed or **taken away**.

Start with
11 counters.

Take away 4.

7 counters
are left.

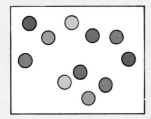 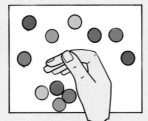 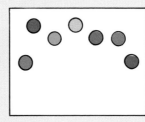

We record this as :
11 − 4 = 7 or 11
$$\begin{array}{r} 11 \\ -\ 4 \\ \hline 7 \end{array}$$

1 Copy and complete these. Use counters or cubes if you need them.

a 14 − 4 =   **c** 15 − 6 =   **e** 16 − 7 =   **g** 19 − 13 =
b 10 − 8 =   **d** 7 − 0 =   **f** 20 − 12 =   **h** 17 − 9 =

2 Copy and fill in the answers. Keep
the figures in straight columns.

a $\begin{array}{r} 8 \\ -5 \\ \hline \end{array}$ **b** $\begin{array}{r} 19 \\ -7 \\ \hline \end{array}$ **c** $\begin{array}{r} 12 \\ -9 \\ \hline \end{array}$ **d** $\begin{array}{r} 16 \\ -10 \\ \hline \end{array}$

3 Record these as you did in question 2.
Keep the figures in straight columns.

a From thirteen take away ten.
b From twenty subtract eighteen.
c From sixteen take away eleven.
d Take eleven away from sixteen.
e From nineteen subtract seven.

Start with
6 ten rods.

Take away
2 ten rods.

4 ten rods
are left.

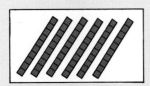 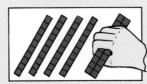 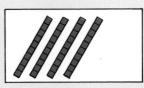

We record
this as :
$$\begin{array}{r} 60 \\ -20 \\ \hline 40 \end{array}$$

4 Copy and complete. Keep the figures in straight columns.

a $\begin{array}{r} 60 \\ -30 \\ \hline \end{array}$ **b** $\begin{array}{r} 40 \\ -20 \\ \hline \end{array}$ **c** $\begin{array}{r} 30 \\ -30 \\ \hline \end{array}$ **d** $\begin{array}{r} 60 \\ -10 \\ \hline \end{array}$ **e** $\begin{array}{r} 40 \\ -40 \\ \hline \end{array}$

Start with 5 tens and 4 units. Take away 2 tens and 1 unit. 3 tens and 3 units are left.

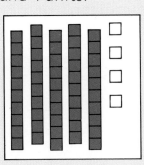 

We record this as:

$$\begin{array}{r} 54 \\ -21 \\ \hline 33 \end{array}$$

1 Estimate first. Use rods if you need them.

a $\begin{array}{r} 37 \\ -23 \\ \hline \end{array}$ **b** $\begin{array}{r} 54 \\ -22 \\ \hline \end{array}$ **c** $\begin{array}{r} 75 \\ -23 \\ \hline \end{array}$ **d** $\begin{array}{r} 68 \\ -46 \\ \hline \end{array}$ **e** $\begin{array}{r} 73 \\ -20 \\ \hline \end{array}$ **f** $\begin{array}{r} 95 \\ -63 \\ \hline \end{array}$

2 Record these as you did in question 1. Keep the figures in straight lines.

a From 36 take 23.   **d** Subtract fifty-two from sixty-four.
b From 49 take 13.   **e** From eighty-eight take twenty-seven.
c From 64 take 52.   **f** Take twenty-seven from eighty-eight.

Counting back

When we use a number line for **addition**, we hop this way : $\oplus \longrightarrow$

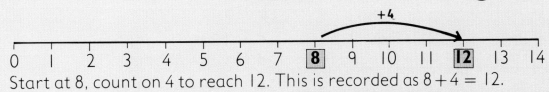

Start at 8, count on 4 to reach 12. This is recorded as $8 + 4 = 12$.

When we use a number line for **subtraction**, we hop this way : $\longleftarrow \ominus$

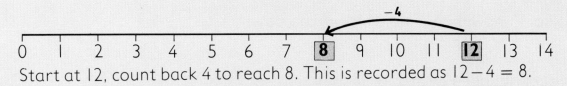

Start at 12, count back 4 to reach 8. This is recorded as $12 - 4 = 8$.

Use a strip of squared paper to make a number line from 0 to 20 like this:

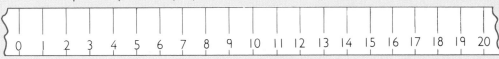

Use your number line to do these.

1   Write the number sentence and put in the missing numeral for ☐

	start at	count back	to reach			start at	count back	to reach
a	12	5	☐	**e**	17	☐	13
b	19	7	☐	**f**	14	14	☐
c	20	12	☐	**g**	16	☐	5
d	10	☐	8	**h**	11	☐	0

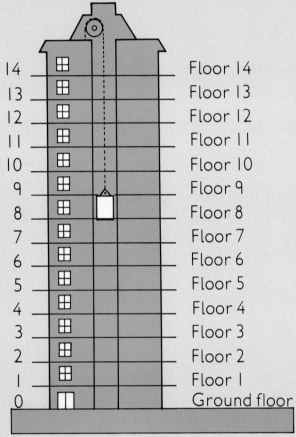

14	Floor 14
13	Floor 13
12	Floor 12
11	Floor 11
10	Floor 10
9	Floor 9
8	Floor 8
7	Floor 7
6	Floor 6
5	Floor 5
4	Floor 4
3	Floor 3
2	Floor 2
1	Floor 1
0	Ground floor

Moving up and down a vertical number line is like using a lift.

The ground floor is called zero or 0.
Going up is like **adding**.
Going down is like **subtracting**.

2   Write a number sentence for each move in this "lift story".

Start at the ground floor and go up 8 floors. $0 + 8 = 8$.
a Now down 5 floors: $8 - 5 = $ ☐
b Go up 11 floors.
c Go down 7 floors.
d Go up 4 floors.
e Which floor are you on now?

3   If you start at floor 13 and go to floor 7, how many floors did you go down? $13 - $ ☐ $= 7$

4   Start at floor 12, go down 8 floors, go up 5 floors.
How many floors must you go down to get to floor 3?

Make up some more "lift stories". Remember the highest floor is number 14 and the lift cannot go below the ground. (There is no basement.)

Chapter 8: Weight 1

Heaviness

When we measure how heavy
things are, we are really
measuring how easy or difficult
it is to pick things up.

1 Try this by lifting different objects.
List them in order of heaviness.
Write down the lightest object first.

The balance

Many years ago
a simple balance was made.
String was tied to the exact
centre of a stick.

This man is comparing
the weight of two fish.
Which is the heavier?
Fish B is heavier than fish A.
Fish A is lighter than fish B.

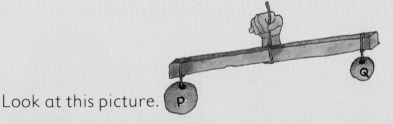

Look at this picture.

Copy these sentences and fill in the gaps.

2 a P is [   ] than Q.   **b** Q is [   ] than P.

   c The heavier weight makes the end of the stick go [   ]

   d The end of the stick with the lighter weight then goes [   ]

Using a school balance

It is important that the arrow is
pointing straight down at the mark
before you start to use the balance.

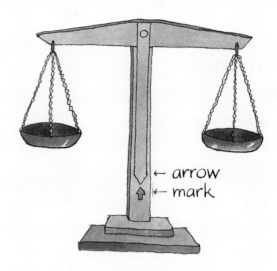

← arrow
← mark

sugar lumps

marbles

pebbles

bottle tops

You can use any of these
objects as weights
but only one kind at a time.

This is how to use the balance
to weigh a lump of clay:

1 Put the lump in one pan.

2 Add marbles one at a time
   to the other pan.

3 When the arrow points
   straight down,
   count the marbles.

Estimating weights

I Hold a large ball of clay in one of your hands.
Take a handful of marbles in the other hand.
Do they feel the same weight?
If not, add or take some away.
Use the balance to check your estimate.
Try another estimate using bottle tops, sugar cubes or pebbles.

2 Make a smaller ball of clay and estimate and weigh again.
Record your estimates and what the balance says, like this:

balances		estimate	school balance
large ball	marbles	10	12
large ball	bottle tops		
large ball	pebbles		

Water in materials

3 Take two jam jars the same size.
Fill one with dry sand, one with damp sand.
Which jar feels heavier?
Check your estimate on the balance.

4 Take a small loaf of fresh bread.
Weigh it on the balance using marbles.
Record how many marbles it weighs.

Do this every day for a week.
Record your results like this:

What is happening to the loaf
of bread? Why is this so?

day	weight in marbles
Monday Tuesday and so on	

Working with modelling clay or Plasticine

 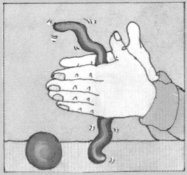 

Try to make two balls
of the same weight.
Check by using
a balance.

Add little bits of
clay to the lighter
ball till they
balance each other.

Make one of the balls
into something long,
like a snake.

Weigh your snake
and the ball
on the balance.

What do you see?

Now make the snake
into a jug.

Weigh the jug and
the ball.

Does the shape of
something change
its weight?

Make some weights out of modelling clay.
It is important that they all weigh the same.
Use the balance to check this.

I Use your weights to weigh
   objects in the classroom.

   Record the weights
   like this:

object	my weights
small book	
shoe	
stone	

2 Borrow your friend's weights.
   Weigh the same objects again.
   Record them next to your own.

   What is wrong with every shop
   using a different set of weights?

   To be fair every shopkeeper
   should use standard weights.
   This means they should
   all be the same.

Kilogram (kg)

One of the standard measures of weight we use today is the kilogram.
We write kg to stand for kilogram.

Hold a 1 kg weight.
Compare it with the weight of objects in the classroom.
Hold each object in your other hand.
Do not use the balance.
Does the object weigh more or less than 1 kg?

1 Record your results like this:

objects heavier than 1 kg	objects lighter than 1 kg
brick reading book	ruler notebook

Less than 1 kg

A kilogram is too heavy to use in shops to weigh anything lighter than a bag of sugar. (This weighs approximately 1 kg.)

There is a smaller standard weight – the gram (g). But this is too light to be useful.
One drawing pin weighs 1 g.

We need something in between.

a kilogram   a gram

What about 500 g?

2 Use the balance to find how many 500 g weights weigh 1 kg.
Copy and complete: 500 g is [ ] a kg.

3 Compare the 500 g weight with objects in the classroom, as you did with the 1 kg weight.
Record in the same way.

Chapter 9: Multiplication 1

1 pack :   4 bars

                  1(4)   = 4

2 packs :   4 + 4   = 8 bars

                  2(4)   = 8

3 packs :   4 + 4 + 4 = 12

                  3(4)   = 12

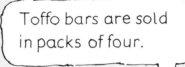

Toffo bars are sold in packs of four.

1   Copy and complete:

    a 5 packs have 4 + 4 + 4 + 4 + 4 = ☐

                           5(4) = ☐

    b 8 packs have [   ] = ☐

                          8(4) = ☐

Draw this table in your book and fill in the squares. →

packs	1	2	3	4	5	6	7	8	9	10
toffo bars	4	8	12							

Four and four and four   4 + 4 + 4 = 12

Three sets of four   3(4) = 12

Five and five and five and five   5 + 5 + 5 + 5 = 20

Four sets of five   4(5) = 20

I Write down the number sentences for these pictures:

a

b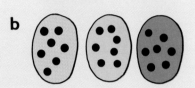

c

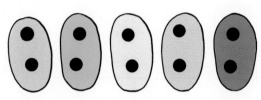

5 sets of 2
5(2) → 10

5 and 2 are the **factors** of 10.
10 is the **product** of 2 and 5 and
we write 2 × 5 = 10.

d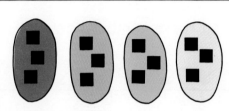

e

f

4 sets of 3
4(3) → 12

3 and 4 are the **factors** of 12.
12 is the **product** of 3 and 4 and
we write 3 × 4 = 12.

2 Copy and write in the products.

a 4 × 2 =	**d** 3 × 5 =	**g** 6 × 3 =	**j** 8 × 1 =	**m** 2 × 2 =
b 2 × 7 =	**e** 4 × 4 =	**h** 5 × 2 =	**k** 3 × 3 =	**n** 5 × 3 =
c 5 × 4 =	**f** 3 × 6 =	**i** 6 × 5 =	**l** 3 × 7 =	**o** 2 × 6 =

3 Copy and fill in the missing factors.

a 2 × ☐ = 6   **e** ☐ × 1 = 8   **i** ☐ × 2 = 4   **m** 7 × ☐ = 14

b ☐ × 5 = 10   **f** 3 × ☐ = 12   **j** 4 × ☐ = 8   **n** ☐ × 5 = 5

c 4 × ☐ = 12   **g** 5 × ☐ = 15   **k** ☐ × 6 = 12   **o** ☐ × 1 = 6

d ☐ × 3 = 15   **h** ☐ × 4 = 16   **l** ☐ × 3 = 9   **p** 2 × ☐ = 16

Hops of the same size

The number line shows $3+3+3+3+3 = 15$

or $\quad 5(3) = 15$

or $\quad 3 \times 5 = 15$

I Look at these number lines and complete the number sentences.

a

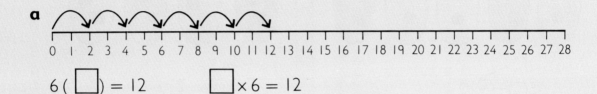

$6(\boxed{}) = 12$ $\qquad \boxed{} \times 6 = 12$

b

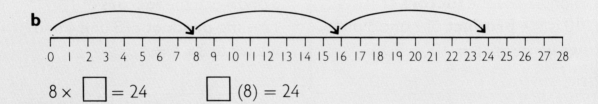

$8 \times \boxed{} = 24$ $\qquad \boxed{}(8) = 24$

c

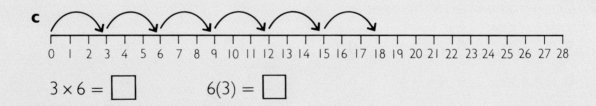

$3 \times 6 = \boxed{}$ $\qquad 6(3) = \boxed{}$

d

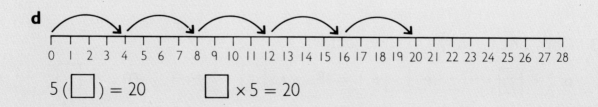

$5(\boxed{}) = 20$ $\qquad \boxed{} \times 5 = 20$

e

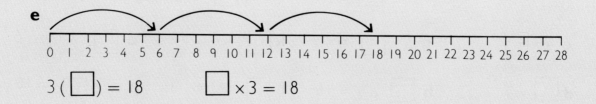

$3(\boxed{}) = 18$ $\qquad \boxed{} \times 3 = 18$

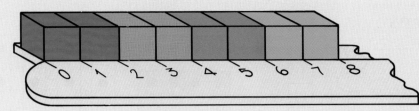

$$2+2+2+2 = 8$$
$$4(2) = 8$$
$$2 \times 4 = 8$$

I Use your own number line or coloured cubes and a number track to complete these.

a $4+4 = \square$

b $2(4) = \square$

c $4 \times 2 = \square$

d $3+3+3+3 = \square$

e $\square (3) = 12$

f $3 \times \square = 12$

g $\square (2) = 10$

h $\square (7) = 14$

i $5 \times 3 = \square$

j $6 \times 4 = \square$

k $5(4) = \square$

l $6 (\square) = 18$

m $8+8+8 = \square$

n $\square (8) = 24$

o $4 \times 4 = \square$

p $5 \times \square = 25$

q $3(\square) = 21$

r $7 \times 3 = \square$

Patterns in multiplication

Ask your teacher for a number grid like this.

Use circles to mark the pattern of 2's and squares to mark the pattern of 4's.

1	②	3	④	5	⑥	7	⑧	9	10
11	12	13	14	15	16	17	18	19	20
21	22	23	24	25	26	27	28	29	30
31	32	33	34	35	36	37	38	39	40
41	42	43	44	45	46	47	48	49	50

On another grid, use triangles to mark the pattern of 3's. Shade in the pattern of 6's.

1	2	△3	4	5	◢6	7	8	△9	10
11	12	13	14	15	16	17	18	19	20
21	22	23	24	25	26	27	28	29	30
31	32	33	34	35	36	37	38	39	40
41	42	43	44	45	46	47	48	49	50

Can you see the pattern of 9's ?

The pattern of 5's is easy to see.
Use another colour to shade it in.

Rows and columns

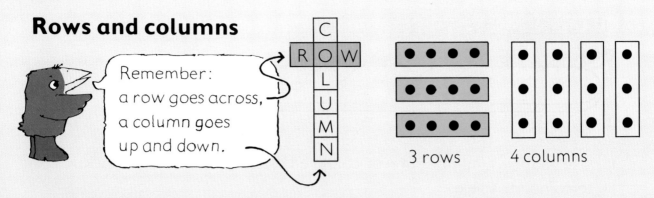

Remember:
a row goes across,
a column goes
up and down.

3 rows   4 columns

15 counters are arranged to make a rectangle:

3 rows of 5 = 15 (5 × 3 = 15)
5 columns of 3 = 15 (3 × 5 = 15)
The product is 15.   The factors are 3 and 5.

1   18 counters are arranged to make a rectangle. Copy and complete.

3 rows of ☐ = 18 (☐ × 3 = 18)
☐ columns of 3 = 18 (3 × ☐ = 18)
The product is . . . . . The factors are . . . . . and . . . . .

2   Make rectangles with :
   a 16 counters   **b** 12 counters   **c** 20 counters   **d** 24 counters
Draw diagrams and record in the same way as the example above.

3   Copy this table
use your answers to
complete it.

Factor	5	6	4	8			4		6		
Factor	3	3			2	3		10	4		
Product	15	18	16	16	12	12	20			24	24

Sometimes a product can be made from more than one pair of factors.

For example:
12 counters can
be arranged as :   or

12 = 3 × 4 = 4 × 3   12 = 2 × 6 = 6 × 2

4   Find as many pairs of factors as you can from these products.
The first one is done for you.
   a 12 = 3 × 4 = 4 × 3 = 2 × 6 = 6 × 2   **b** 16   **c** 18   **d** 24   **e** 36

Chapter 10: Time 1

Counting minutes in fives

outside
/ minutes

inside hours

A clock face like this has an inside part and an outside part.

The inside part has numbers for counting hours.
The outside part is split up by 60 short lines.
These lines stand for minutes.
The long minute hand of the clock
goes round all the lines in 60 minutes.

one, two, three, four, five, six, seven, eight, nine . . . .

To find how many minutes have gone by,
you could count how many lines
the minute hand has passed.
It is easier to use the thick lines to
count in fives – 5, 10, 15, 20 . . .
The minute hand of this clock
is pointing at the 25 minute mark.

Use a rubber stamp to print a clock face.
Put all the five minute numbers
round the edge like this.

The line at the top is both for 0 and 60.

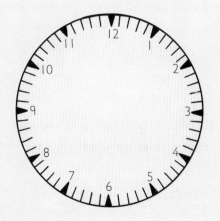

1 Look at this clock face with letters around it:

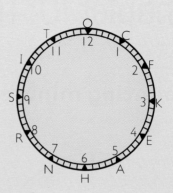

2 Write the letters that are
by the following five minute numbers.
It will make a sentence. What does it say?

10	25	45	55		30	60	40	45	20	45
40	25	5	20		25	55		55	30	20
55	40	25	5	15						

3 Use the letters round the clock face to make a message.
Change each letter to the number next to it. Ask a friend to work it out.

Often you need to start counting minutes
from different marks on the clock face.

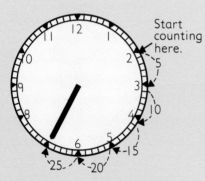

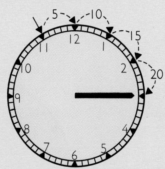

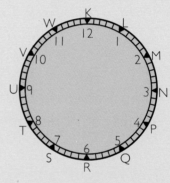

Count five-minute
marks round
the edge from
the starting point.

The time shown here
is 25 minutes after
the 10 minute mark.

You can start from
anywhere.

This time is
20 minutes after
the 55 minute mark.

Use this clock face
to answer
the questions below.

Remember the hand
always moves
the same way.

4 How many minutes does it take:

a from M to R   **c** from Q to K   **e** from V to M   **g** from S to N
b from P to U   **d** from W to L   **f** from T to P   **h** from R to Q

5 Make up some more questions like these.

1 Think of a clock face as something you can slice up, like a cake.
How many minutes long are these slices?
Write the answers in your book.

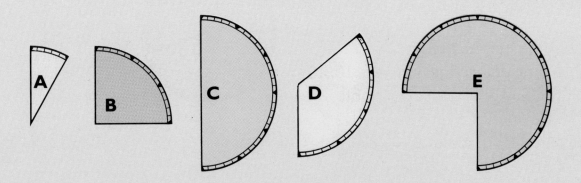

Fractions of an hour

The minute hand goes right round the clock face in 60 minutes.
60 minutes is 1 hour. So 30 minutes is half ($\frac{1}{2}$) an hour.

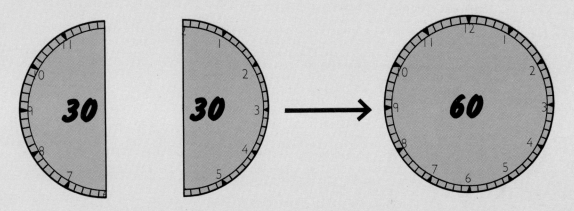

2 Write these sentences in your book and fill in the gaps.
The shaded clock faces below will help you.

a 15 mins. is ☐ of an hour.
b 15 mins. + 15 mins. + ☐ mins. = 45 mins.
c 45 mins. is ☐ of an hour.
d 45 mins. + $\frac{1}{4}$ of an hour = ☐ hour.
e 20 mins. + 40 mins. = ☐ hour.
f 20 mins. + 20 mins. + ☐ mins. = 1 hour.
g A third of an hour is ☐ mins.

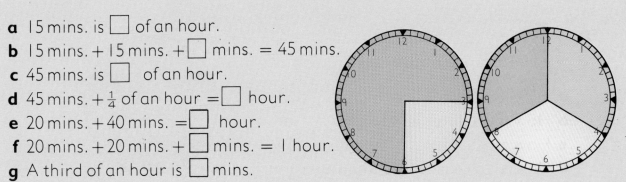

Counting on the small lines

This clock shows that 18 minutes have passed.

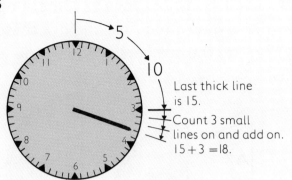

Last thick line is 15.

Count 3 small lines on and add on. 15+3 =18.

Count in fives to the last thick line before the hand – 5, 10, 15 Now count the number of small minute lines up to the hand – 1,2,3. 15 minutes + 3 minutes = 18 minutes.

1 a How many minutes are there between the 0 mark and the P?
   b How much later is Q than the 5 minute mark?
   c How much earlier is the 20 minute mark than R?
   d How much later is S than the 55 minute mark?

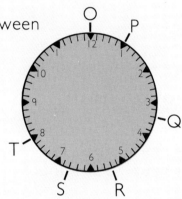

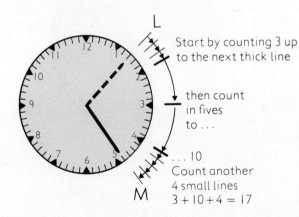

Start by counting 3 up to the next thick line

then count in fives to...

... 10 Count another 4 small lines 3+10+4 = 17

To count the time from a small time, count minutes from the start to the first thick line. Add these minutes to any extra minutes at the end.

2 Look at this clock face marked with letters and answer these questions:

   a How much later is W than V?
   b How much later is X than W?
   c How much later is Y than X?
   d How much earlier is Z than V?

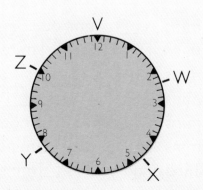

Chapter 11: Capacity 1

Which holds the most?

Greedy Sam always wants the most.

How can he find which cup
holds the most?
Is it the tallest or the widest?

1   Take four cups that look different.
    Fill them with water to compare how much they hold.
    List them in order.

2   Some shampoo comes in trick bottles.
    Bring some empty shampoo bottles
    to school.

    Fill them with water
    to see which one holds the most.

    Why are they trick bottles?

3   You can compare boxes too.

    Estimate which box is largest,
    second largest, and so on.
    List your estimates.

    Fill the boxes with sand
    and compare them.
    Were you right? Record the results.

Measuring capacity

To measure the capacity of a container, you put liquid, dry sand or rice into it. Capacity is how much a container holds.

If a container is tall it does not mean that it holds more than a short one.

Use the cups, bottles and boxes you had before. Find an egg cup to use as a measure.

1 List your containers and your findings like this:

container.	estimate (eggcupfuls)	measure (eggcupfuls)
cup 1	10	
cup 2	8	

Fill the eggcup with water and use it to fill the cups.

Fill the shampoo bottle and see how many times it will fill the eggcup.

Use sand for the box. Level off each eggcupful with your finger, then pour it into the box.

Choosing a measure

Sometimes we have to measure the capacity of large and small containers.

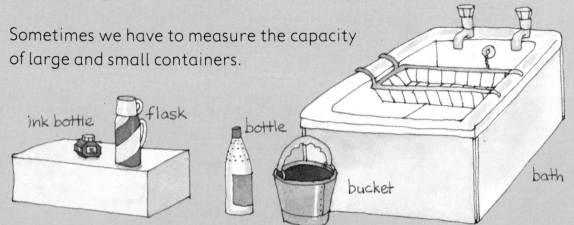

1 **a** Imagine you need to measure the capacity of all the things above.
Which measure would you choose from the ones below?

b Record your choice like this:

to measure	I would use
bath	
bucket	
ink bottle	
flask bottle	

Strange things about some containers

2 **a** Find four containers that are very different shapes.
Pour a cupful of water into each container. Draw a line on the side of the containers to mark the water level.

b Tilt each container in turn. What happens to the water level?

c Make a drawing of an upright container and show the water level.
Then draw it tilted. Show the water level again.

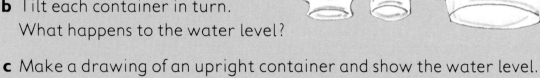

Chapter 12: Division 1

Sharing equally

12 cakes to be shared equally between 4 plates.

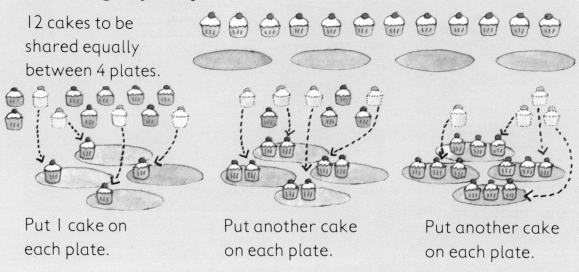

Put 1 cake on each plate.

Put another cake on each plate.

Put another cake on each plate.

12 cakes shared equally on 4 plates – 3 cakes on each plate.

The set of 12 cakes is divided to make 4 sub-sets with 3 in each sub-set.

Dividing means splitting a set into equal sub-sets.
We say: 12 divided by 4 is 3. We write: $12 \div 4 = 3$.

÷ means divided by

1   Mrs Brown says to her 4 children, "Divide this bar of chocolate equally between you."
    Draw the bar and the pieces each child should have.

2   Take 10 counters or cubes and put them in 2 equal rows.

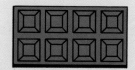

Draw the rows of counters.
Under your picture copy and complete.
There are ⬜ in each row. $10 \div 2 = $ ⬜

3   Put 24 counters or cubes in 3 equal columns. Draw the columns.
    Under your picture copy and complete:
    There are ⬜ in each column. $24 \div 3 = $ ⬜

I Use counters or cubes to answer these in the same way.
Record the answers in your book.

a Put 18 in 3 equal columns.
There are ☐ in each column.
18 ÷ 3 = ☐

c Put 15 in 3 equal rows.
There are ☐ in each row.
15 ÷ 3 = ☐

b Put 16 in 2 equal rows.
There are ☐ in each row.
16 ÷ 2 = ☐

d Put 30 in 5 equal columns.
There are ☐ in each column.
30 ÷ 5 = ☐

2 Look carefully at these patterns.
Copy and complete the sentences under each.

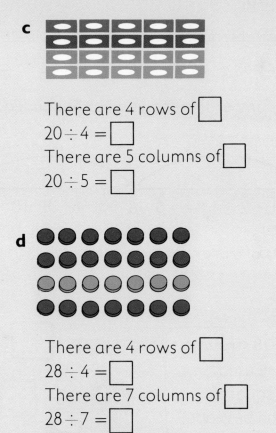

a

There are 6 columns of ☐
12 ÷ 6 = ☐
There are 2 rows of ☐
12 ÷ 2 = ☐

b

There are 3 columns of ☐
15 ÷ 3 = ☐
There are 5 rows of ☐
15 ÷ 5 = ☐

c

There are 4 rows of ☐
20 ÷ 4 = ☐
There are 5 columns of ☐
20 ÷ 5 = ☐

d

There are 4 rows of ☐
28 ÷ 4 = ☐
There are 7 columns of ☐
28 ÷ 7 = ☐

3 Estimate first. Use counters or cubes if you need them.

a 18 ÷ 3 =   **e** 16 ÷ 4 =   **i** 18 ÷ 9 =   **m** 30 ÷ 10 =
b 24 ÷ 6 =   **f** 25 ÷ 5 =   **j** 28 ÷ 4 =   **n** 32 ÷ 8 =
c 30 ÷ 6 =   **g** 12 ÷ 4 =   **k** 14 ÷ 2 =   **o** 24 ÷ 3 =
d 21 ÷ 7 =   **h** 36 ÷ 6 =   **l** 20 ÷ 5 =   **p** 28 ÷ 7 =

Division by repeated subtraction

Start with 18 marbles.

Take away 6 marbles and put them in a bag.

That leaves 12 marbles.

Take away 6 marbles and put them in a bag.

That leaves 6 marbles. ⬭

Take away 6 marbles and put them in a bag. ⬭

that leaves 0 marbles.

18 marbles have been put into 3 bags with 6 marbles in each bag

6 was subtracted 3 times   6 in a bag, 3 bags.

$18 \div 6 = 3$ $6 \times 3 = 18.$

The number line shows what happened :

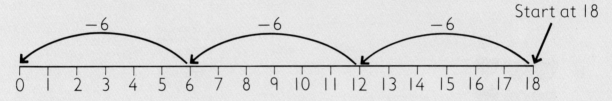

3 lots of 6 are subtracted. $18 \div 6 = 3$

If 28 straws
are used,
7 squares
can be made.

$28 \div 4 = 7$

1   Use some straws to make squares. Copy and complete.

a $20 \div 4 =$ **c** $12 \div 4 =$ **e** $4 \div 4 =$ **g** $36 \div 4 =$

b $8 \div 4 =$ **d** $24 \div 4 =$ **f** $32 \div 4 =$ **h** $16 \div 4 =$

This set of 20 counters can be divided into sub-sets with 5 in each.

 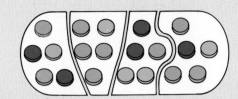

When 20 counters are put in five's
there are 4 sub-sets. $20 \div 5 = 4$

I Estimate first, then use counters to find how many sub-sets.

    a 12 divided into sub-sets with 6 in each.
      $12 \div 6 =$ ☐

    b 24 divided into sub-sets with 8 in each.
      $24 \div 8 =$ ☐

    c 18 divided into sub-sets with 9 in each.
      $18 \div 9 =$ ☐

    d 30 divided into sub-sets with 10 in each.
      $30 \div 10 =$ ☐

    e 28 divided into sub-sets with 7 in each.
      $28 \div 7 =$ ☐

    f 16 divided into sub-sets with 4 in each.
      $16 \div 4 =$ ☐

    g 32 divided into sub-sets with 8 in each.
      $32 \div 8 =$ ☐

    h 27 divided into sub-sets with 9 in each.
      $27 \div 9 =$ ☐

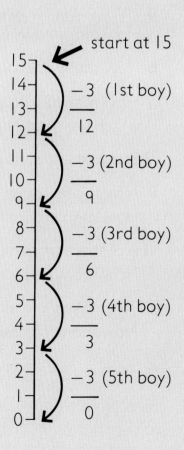

Some boys were given 3 apples each.
If 15 apples were given away,
how many boys received apples?
This can be worked out on a number line. ➡

Starting at 15 and hopping in
threes, it takes 5 hops to reach 0.

So 5 boys will receive 3 apples each.

1 Use your number line for these:

a $30 \div 10 = \square$ **c** $24 \div 6 = \square$ **e** $18 \div 3 = \square$

b $27 \div 3 = \square$ **d** $28 \div 7 = \square$ **f** $36 \div 6 = \square$

2 Estimate first, then use the number line to answer these:

a If a coat has 6 buttons, how many coats will have been made when 30 buttons have been used?

b Rubbers cost 7p each. How many can be bought for 35p?

c Mother gave each of her children £5, if she gave away £25 how many children has she?

d There are 4 children to each table in the dining hall, if 32 children stayed to lunch how many tables were used?

e How many pieces of ribbon each 8 centimetres long can be cut from a length of 24 centimetres?

f There are 18 children working in pairs on a project. How many pairs are there?

g For a concert, 36 chairs are put into rows with 9 in a row. How many rows will there be?

h How many chocolate bars at 5p each can you buy for 30p?

i How many 2 kilogram weights will balance a parcel which weighs 12 kg?

j Stacked in 6's, how many stacks will 24 chairs make?

k A medicine spoon holds 5 millilitres. How many spoonfuls can be poured from 35 millilitres?

l 4 of these ▽ triangles make a square ⊠ How many squares can be made from 36 triangles?

m John takes 9 seconds to sharpen a pencil. How many can he sharpen in 27 seconds?

Chapter 13: Addresses

This picture shows the lockers in a classroom.

Fred says, "To find my locker start at the bottom corner on the left, count 4 lockers across and 3 lockers up."

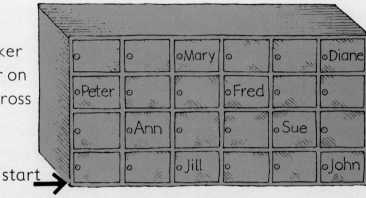

If we always start at the bottom left corner   count across first   then up.

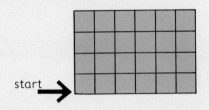 

We can say where a locker is by using two numbers with a comma betwen them: (4,3).

The first number tells you how many **across**, the second number tells you how many **up**.

(4,3) is the address of Fred's locker.

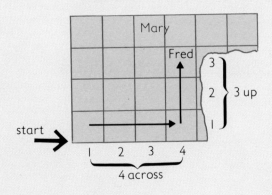

Keep to the order: across, up.

(4,3) is Fred's locker;   (3,4) is Mary's locker.

1 Write in your book the address of:

    a Jill's locker   **d** Peter's locker   **g** the locker underneath Sue's

    b Ann's locker   **e** John's locker   **h** The locker next to Diane's.

    c Sue's locker   **f** Diane's locker

2 Draw a block of lockers on a piece of squared paper.
Mark the bottom left corner of the lockers as START.
Write the names of your friends on the lockers.
Make a list of the names and addresses of each friend's locker.

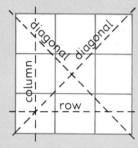

A game of Noughts and Crosses is won by
the first player to get either a row,
column or diagonal of noughts (O) or crosses (X).

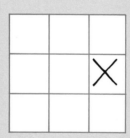

Copy this grid on to squared paper.
The position of the X marked in this picture is (3,2)

The rest of the X's in the game are at (3,3) (1,3) (1,1)
and the O's are in the positions (2,2), (3,1) (2,3) (2,1).
Mark these on your grid.

3 In your book write:
    a Who has won the game, O or X?   **b** Which square is empty?

4 Draw some more diagrams on squared paper and find the winners
of these two games. Write your answers in your book.

    a John X's at (1,1) (1,3) (3,1) (2,1)
       Tom O's at (3,3) (1,2) (2,2)

    b Mary X's at (2,2) (3,1) (1,2) (2,3)
       Ann O's at (1,1) (1,3) (3,2) (2,1)

Naming squares on a map

This is a map of a village. The columns and rows are numbered
so that we can give the address
of each place on the map.

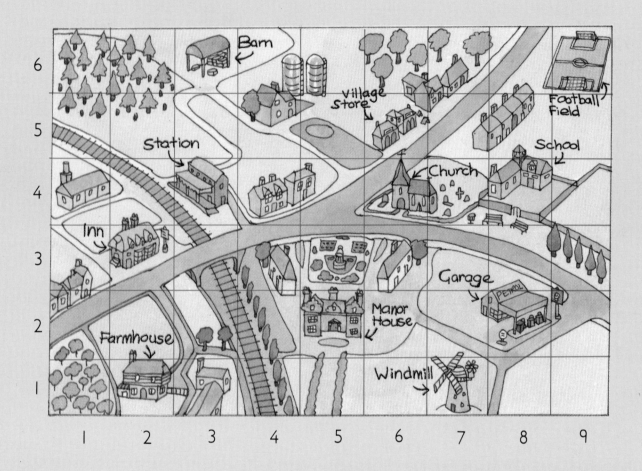

1   Copy and complete this list of addresses. The first one is done for you.

a Manor house (5,2)	**e** Barn	**i** Village store
b Windmill	**f** Station	**j** Church
c School	**g** Farmhouse	**k** Football field
d Bridge	**h** Inn	**l** Garage

On squared paper draw a map of your own.
Make a list of the places
you have put on your map. Write the address of each.

Codes

We can use the addresses
of squares to write messages
in a secret code.

F is in square (1,4)

O is in square (5,3)

X is in square (4,1)

So "FOX" is written in code
as (1,4) (5,3) (4,1)

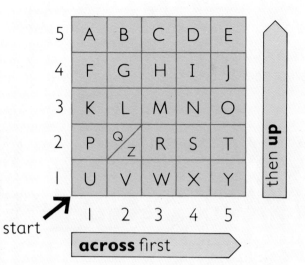

1 Write in your book what this message says:
   (1,5)   (3,4) (1,5) (1,2) (1,2) (5,1)   (4,5) (5,3) (2,4)
   (3,1) (1,5) (2,4) (4,2)   (4,4) (5,2) (4,2)   (5,2) (1,5) (4,4) (2,3)

2 Write the message COME NEXT WEEK in code.

3 Make up some more coded messages for your friends to decode.

These shapes are needed for questions 3 and 4
on the opposite page.

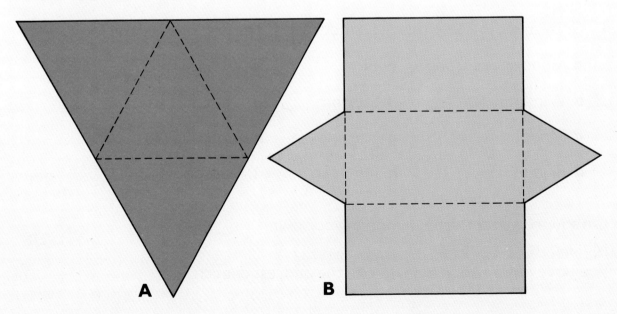

A   B

Chapter 14: Shape 2

These objects are called solids. The outside, or skin, of a solid is called its surface.

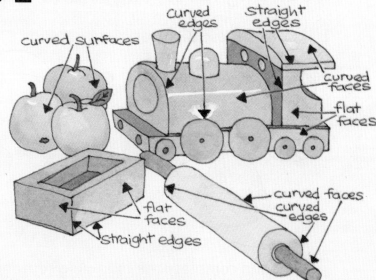

I Copy these sentences.
To fill the blanks use a word from this list:

| flat |
| straight |
| curved |

   a The apples have [＿＿＿＿] surfaces.

   b The brick has [＿＿＿＿] faces and [＿＿＿＿] edges.

   c The rolling pin has [＿＿＿＿] faces and [＿＿＿＿] edges.

   d The toy engine has both [＿＿＿＿] and [＿＿＿＿] faces;
   some edges are [＿＿＿＿] and some are [＿＿＿＿]

2 Using straws and pieces of pipe cleaners we can make the framework or skeleton of a solid.

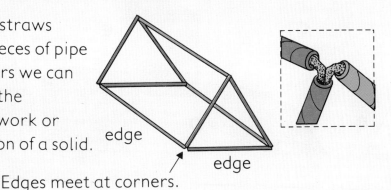

edge

edge

Edges meet at corners.

3 Copy and cut out shape "A" shown on page 62.
Fold along the dotted lines
to make a solid shape like this:
Stick it together with Sellotape.

4 Do the same with shape "B" shown
on page 62. Fold it along the dotted lines
to get a solid like this one.

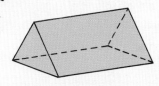

Counting faces, edges and corners

I Look at these pictures of some solids.

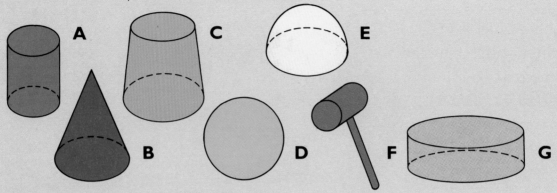

Copy and complete the following sentences.
The first one is done for you.
a The solids with 3 faces are `A, C, G`
b The solids with 2 faces are ⬚
c The solids with I surface are ⬚
d The solids with 2 curved edges are ⬚
e The solids with I flat surface are ⬚

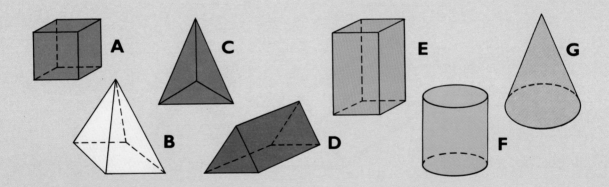

2 Copy and complete

name of solid	faces	edges	corners
A cube	6		
B square pyramid			
C triangular pyramid			
D triangular prism		9	
E cuboid			
F cylinder			0
G cone	2		

I Look carefully at these pictures of solid shapes.
Remember, there may be some faces, edges or corners you can't see.

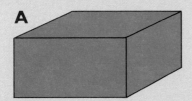

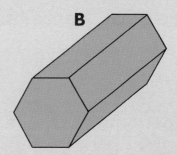

2 a Which shape has only one square face?
  b How many faces has shape **A**?
  c What shape is the face with six edges in **B**?
  d How many triangular faces does shape **C** have?
  e How many edges has shape **B**?
  f How many corners has shape **C**?

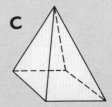

The shape that a solid stands on is called a base.
  g What shape is the base of shape **A**?
  h What shape is the base of shape **B**?

3 a Make sets of solids which are all the same shape and size.

  b Try to fit the solids in each set together.
   Make a list of the solids which fit
   together without spaces between.

  c Which of these objects can be packed in a box
   without spaces between? Make a list.

   Sugar cubes, eggs, marbles, matchboxes, sticks of chalk,
   oranges, cornflake boxes, tins of soup.

Chapter 15: Subtraction 2

Subtraction patterns

You can use a table like this
for subtraction:

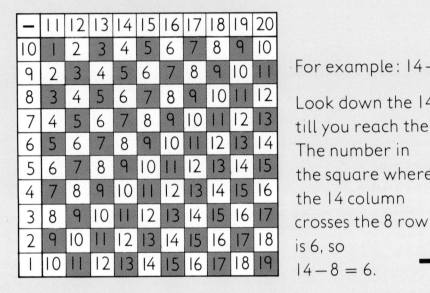

For example: $14 - 8 = \Box$

Look down the 14 column
till you reach the 8 row.
The number in
the square where
the 14 column
crosses the 8 row
is 6, so
$14 - 8 = 6$.

I Use this table to answer these:

a	b	c	d
14 − 6	17 − 9	16 − 7	19 − 8
16 − 4	15 − 7	18 − 5	15 − 6
18 − 10	19 − 5	14 − 3	11 − 10
20 − 2	13 − 9	12 − 9	19 − 2

Look for patterns in the subtraction table.

Even numbers can all be divided by 2 without a remainder:
2, 4, 6, 8, 10, 12, 14, 16, 18, 20, 22, . . .

Odd numbers have a remainder of 1 when divided by 2:
3, 5, 7, 9, 11, 13, 15, 17, 19, 21, 23, . . .

What do you notice about the answers in a?
What about the answers in b, c and d?

The computer

The pointers
on the computer
say −3
so it will subtract 3
from each number
fed into the input

The computer records all the inputs and outputs on
a print-out tape:

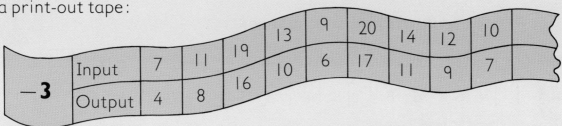

−3	Input	7	11	19	13	9	20	14	12	10
				16	10	6	17	11	9	7
	Output	4	8							

Check the tape to see if the computer is working properly.
As an odd number is being subtracted, check that odd − odd = even
and even − odd = odd.

I Look for patterns to help you estimate.
Copy and complete these tapes:

a

−6	9	19	29	39	49	12	22	32	42	52

b

−8	10	20	30	40	50	13	23	33	43	53

c

−9	14	24	34	15	25	35	16	26	36	46

d

−13	20	30	40	50	60	70	80	90

e

−5	13	18	23	28	35	38	43	48

2 Make up some more tapes of your own.

Making up the difference

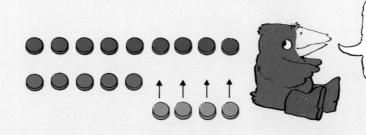

"What is the **difference between** 9 and 5?" can be written like this . . .

$$9 - 5 = \boxed{}$$

Remember to estimate first.

Another way of asking this question is:

"What must I add on to 5 to make a total of 9" or "5 and what makes 9?"

I Copy these and fill in the missing number.

a $9 + \boxed{} = 12$ **c** $11 + \boxed{} = 19$ **e** $7 + \boxed{} = 15$ **g** $11 + \boxed{} = 17$

b $5 + \boxed{} = 16$ **d** $8 + \boxed{} = 14$ **f** $17 + \boxed{} = 20$ **h** $8 + \boxed{} = 20$

To make up the difference between larger numbers we can add on in steps.
For example:
"What must be added to 28 to make a total of 50?" $28 + \boxed{} = 50$

Write the smaller number first, leave a gap and then write the larger number. Add on in steps. Write the numbers added in each step. Add the "steps".

$$28 \qquad\qquad\qquad 50$$
$$28 \rightarrow 30 \rightarrow 40 \rightarrow 50$$
$$2 + \underbrace{10 + 10}$$
$$20$$
$$2$$
$$\overline{22}$$

$28 + 22 = 50$ or $50 - 28 = 22$

Another way of setting this out uses a zig-zag pattern.

$$28$$
$$\qquad 2 \qquad \text{28 up to 30 is 2}$$
$$30$$
$$\qquad 10 \qquad \text{30 up to 40 is 10}$$
$$40$$
$$\qquad 10 \qquad \text{40 up to 50 is 10}$$
$$50$$
$$\overline{22}$$

This method is like giving change for 50p when sweets costing 28p are bought:

"28 pence . . .   30 . . .   40 . . .   50 pence."

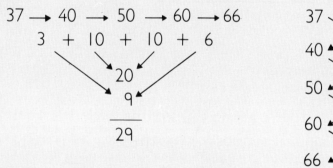

The total change is 22p.

The shopkeeper gives you the change by counting on from the price up to the money you gave him.

Here is another example: $37 + \boxed{} = 66$

$$37 \rightarrow 40 \rightarrow 50 \rightarrow 60 \rightarrow 66$$
$$3 + 10 + 10 + 6$$
$$20$$
$$9$$
$$\overline{29}$$

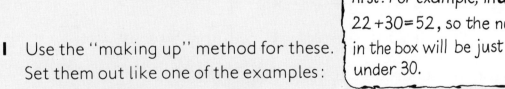

$37 + 29 = 66$ or $66 - 37 = 29$

Think about the answer first. For example, in **a**, $22 + 30 = 52$, so the number in the box will be just under 30.

l Use the "making up" method for these. Set them out like one of the examples:

a $22 + \boxed{} = 50$ **e** $13 + \boxed{} = 51$ **i** $69 + \boxed{} = 86$ **m** $34 + \boxed{} = 72$

b $25 + \boxed{} = 60$ **f** $43 + \boxed{} = 86$ **j** $38 + \boxed{} = 66$ **n** $9 + \boxed{} = 27$

c $34 + \boxed{} = 70$ **g** $23 + \boxed{} = 62$ **k** $46 + \boxed{} = 75$ **o** $11 + \boxed{} = 50$

d $19 + \boxed{} = 42$ **h** $48 + \boxed{} = 71$ **l** $55 + \boxed{} = 93$ **p** $24 + \boxed{} = 83$

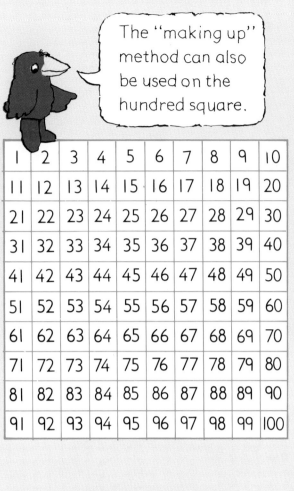

The "making up" method can also be used on the hundred square.

Each hop this way ▢▢ adds on 1.

Each hop this way ▢ adds on 10.

From 5 up to 9 is 4 hops this way

5 6 7 8 9   5 + ▢4 = 9

From 12 up to 42 is 3 hops this way
12
22
32
42

From 26 to 50

4 hops this way
and 2 hops this way

26 27 28 29 30
40
50

4
+20
24

26 + ▢24 = 50

1 Estimate first, then use the 100 square with "unit hops" and "ten hops" for these.

a 3 + ▢ = 9   **e** 13 + ▢ = 23   **i** 8 + ▢ = 15   **m** 31 + ▢ = 70

b 2 + ▢ = 10   **f** 47 + ▢ = 67   **j** 28 + ▢ = 40   **n** 28 + ▢ = 90

c 20 + ▢ = 50   **g** 10 + ▢ = 14   **k** 37 + ▢ = 80   **o** 14 + ▢ = 80

d 40 + ▢ = 90   **h** 20 + ▢ = 27   **l** 56 + ▢ = 90   **p** 29 + ▢ = 41

You can use the hundred square for "taking away" as well as "making up".

What does I hop this way ▢▢ mean?   What does I hop this way ▢ mean?

2 Rewrite the "making up" questions as "take aways" and check them on the 100 square. For example, rewrite 3 + ▢ = 9 as 9 − 3 = ▢

Word problems

Word problems are like stories which have to be
changed into number sentences.

John has
12 marbles.

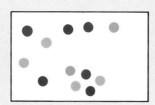

He loses
5 marbles.

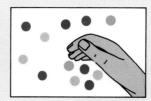

How many are left? 12 − 5 =   This is a "take away" problem.

In a sale, the price of a jig-saw is reduced from 65p to 44p.

1 How much cheaper
is it in the sale?
This is a "difference"
problem.

65p (old price)
44p (new price)
___ p cheaper

2 By the end of a netball match,
Jenny's team had scored 28 goals.
If 17 were scored in the first half,
how many were scored in
the second half?

1st half	2nd half	total
17	?	28

This is a "make up to" problem.

3 Remember to estimate first.

  a Mrs Giles had 18 eggs. She sold 12. How many were left?

  b Peter collected 23 conkers but he lost 10. How many are left?

  c Susan wants to save 45p to buy a book.
  So far she has saved 32p. How much more does she need?

  d Alison weighs 35 kilograms and is 14 kilograms
  heavier than Betty. How much does Betty weigh?

  e Mary did a jig-saw in 40 minutes but Jane did hers
  13 minutes faster. How long did Jane take?

  f On a hot day Mr. Jones sold 20 litres of ice-cream. On a cold
  day he sold 9 litres. How much more did he sell on a hot day?

  g Carol's pace is 50 centimetres long, her handspan is 16
  centimetres. How much longer is her pace than her handspan?

Chapter 16: Money 2

5p coins

To help you count these
5p coins you need to
know how to count in fives.

Do you remember this
pattern? If not – learn it.

| 5 | 10 | 15 | 20 | 25 | 30 | 35 | 40 | 45 | 50 |

1 Counting in fives. In your book record
the total amount
of each
of these.

a  → ☐ b → ☐

c → ☐ d → ☐

Some people
like to
count their
5p coins
in pairs,
for example:

↓   ↓   ↓   ↓

10p   +   10p   +   10p   +   5p → **35p**

2 Take some 5 pence coins, use them to do these,
remember to sort into pairs. Write the answers in your book.
The first one is done for you.

a 8 coins → 40p   **c** 6 coins → ☐

b 5 coins → ☐   **d** 9 coins → ☐

Finding the total value of mixed coins

John has some coins:

To help him find their total value he puts them
in order starting with the coin of highest value.

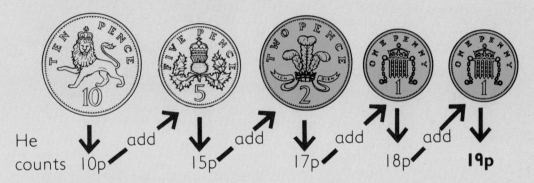

He
counts   10p   15p   17p   18p   **19p**

He records this as: 10p, 15p, 17p, 18p, 19p.

1 Do these, recording your answers in the same way.
   Remember to use your coins, sort them and then find the total.

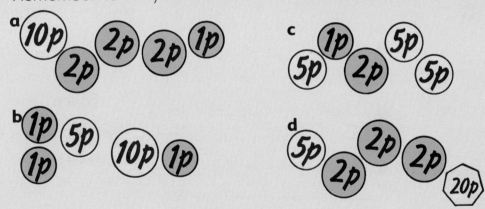

2 Use your coins to do these in the same way. You will need coins for
   the values given. Sort them first and then record your answers.

   a 2p, 1p, 10p, 2p.   **d** 2p, 5p, 10p, 2p, 1p, 20p, 5p, 10p.
   b 1p, 10p, 2p, 5p, 1p.   **e** 1p, 10p, 5p, 2p, 5p, 10p, 1p, 20p.
   c 1p, 5p, 2p, 10p, 1p.

   Take some more coins, sort them into order and find the total.

Going shopping

1 Look at the shop.

   a What is the cheapest
item on sale?

   b How much is the least
expensive ice cream?

   c How much more
expensive is home-made
toffee than ordinary toffee?

   d How much do you save by buying
a pencil instead of a ball point?

2 Remember to estimate first.

Copy these bills filling in the prices from the picture of the shop.
Use coins to find the total amount of each bill.
The first one is done for you.

   a Toffee 9p
      Mints   4p
           13p

   e Choc-bar
     Choc-drops

   i Felt pen
    Fruits

   m Choc-bar
      Crayons
      Ball point pen

   b Large ice cream
     Orange drink

   f Felt pen
    Humbugs

   j Choc-drops
    Fruits

   n Pencil
    Note book
    Toffee

   c Ball point pen
    Note book

   g Toffee
    Liquorice

   k Choc-drops
    Liquorice

   o Liquorice
    Mints
    Choc-drops

   d Pencil
    Crayons

   h Mints
    Choc-drops

   l Fruits
    Liquorice

3 Find the cost of these: Now try these:

   a 2 pencils at 6p each
   b 5 small ice creams
   c 4 packets of humbugs
   d 4 note books
   e 8 packets of mints

   f How many packets of humbugs can
I buy for 12p?

   g How many packets of crayons can
I buy for 30p?

   h How many packets of mints can I buy for 24p?

Giving change up to 50p

I spend 36p in a shop
and give the shopkeeper 50p.
He gives me the change this way:

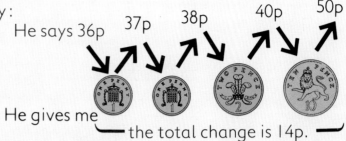

He says 36p   37p   38p   40p   50p

He gives me

the total change is 14p.

1 What change from 50p do I get if I spend these amounts?
Use coins and list them.

a 41p	**d** 23p	**g** 44p	**j** 5p
b 35p	**e** 12p	**h** 14p	**k** 17p
c 31p	**f** 8p	**i** 29p	**l** 33p

Giving change (selecting coins offered)

In my purse
I have:

I buy a bar of toffee which costs 9p.
I cannot give the correct amount.
I can give 10p and have 1p change.

I could record this as:

amount given	10p
price of toffee	9p
change	1p

2 Show how you might pay for these using the coins in the purse only.
Record your answers as above.

a A ball which costs 34p.   **e** A book which costs 45p.

b A pen which costs 24p.   **f** A pencil which costs 4p.

c A note book which costs 14p.   **g** A toy car which costs 69p.

d A kite which costs 79p.   **h** A game which costs 84p.

Looking at change given

1 You go
to a shop
with 20p. You are
given
2p change. How much
did
you spend?

Write how much you spent in your book.

2 Take to the shop: Change:

a

b

c

d

e

f

The cost of household goods

Do you know what your family pays for these?
Find out tonight and record your prices tomorrow.

3 Write in your book the answers to these.
What change would you get from 50p if you bought:

a A kilogram of sugar   **d** A bottle of milk

b A loaf   **e** Six eggs

c A packet of cornflakes   **f** A tablet of soap

Chapter 17: Multiplication 2

More rows and columns

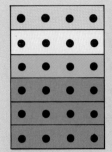
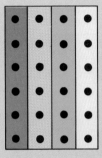

6 rows of 4   4 columns of 6
6(4)   4(6) $4 \times 6 = 24 = 6 \times 4$

I Copy the number sentence and fill in the missing numbers for these:

a

$\square \times \triangle = \square = \triangle \times \square$

b

$\square \times \triangle = \square = \triangle \times \square$

c

$\square \times \triangle = \square = \triangle \times \square$

d

$\square \times \triangle = \square = \triangle \times \square$

2 Copy and complete. Use counters or pegs if you wish.

a $4 \times 3 =$	**e** $5 \times 6 =$	**i** $8 \times 3 =$	**m** $4 \times 8 =$	**q** $9 \times 3 =$
b $3 \times 4 =$	**f** $6 \times 5 =$	**j** $3 \times 8 =$	**n** $8 \times 4 =$	**r** $3 \times 9 =$
c $5 \times 3 =$	**g** $3 \times 7 =$	**k** $9 \times 2 =$	**o** $4 \times 7 =$	**s** $7 \times 5 =$
d $3 \times 5 =$	**h** $7 \times 3 =$	**l** $2 \times 9 =$	**p** $7 \times 4 =$	**t** $5 \times 7 =$

Two factors multiplied in any order give the same product.

Square numbers

If the number of rows and the number of columns is the same,
you have a **square number**.

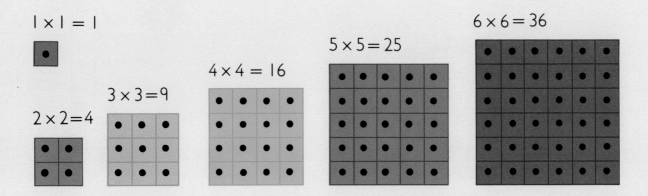

$1 \times 1 = 1$

$2 \times 2 = 4$

$3 \times 3 = 9$

$4 \times 4 = 16$

$5 \times 5 = 25$

$6 \times 6 = 36$

1, 4, 9, 16, 25, 36 are all square numbers

What are the next two square numbers after 36?

Make pictures of square numbers by colouring in squared paper
or by using elastic bands on a geoboard

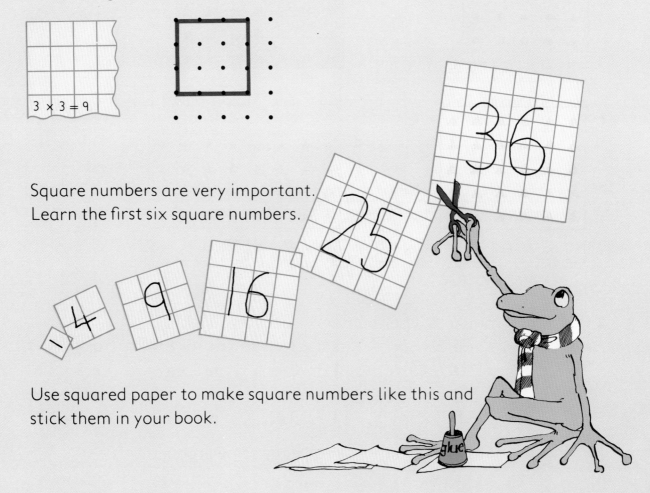

$3 \times 3 = 9$

Square numbers are very important.
Learn the first six square numbers.

Use squared paper to make square numbers like this and
stick them in your book.

Learning multiplication tables – making a start

Learning your tables helps you to find products quickly.

Try to know them as well as you know your name.

Make a start by learning the products from 1 x 1 up to 6 x 6.

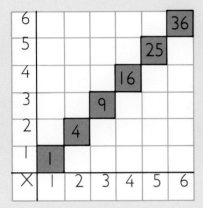

The square numbers make a diagonal.

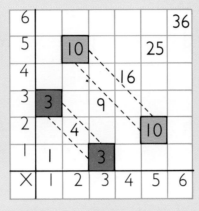

Because 1 x 3 = 3 x 1, 5 x 2 = 2 x 5 etc.

We only need to fill in the spaces on one side of the diagonal.

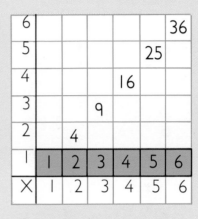

The table of 1's is easy.

Any number multiplied by 1 is itself.

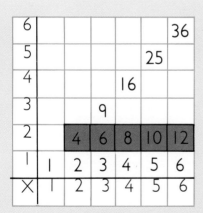

Doubling gives you the table of 2's.

This leaves:

4 x 3 = 12   6 x 3 = 18
5 x 3 = 15   6 x 4 = 24
5 x 4 = 20   6 x 5 = 30

Use squared paper to make your own multiplication square up to 6 x 6.

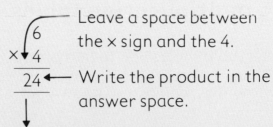

Leave a space between the × sign and the 4.

Write the product in the answer space.

The 2 stands for "2 tens" so it should be in a separate column.

1 Copy and complete these:

a	5	d	4	g	2	j	4	m	6	p	4
	× 2		× 3		× 6		× 5		× 5		× 1

b	6	e	5	h	4	k	6	n	5	q	3
	× 3		× 6		× 4		× 1		× 5		× 4

c	10	f	6	i	10	l	3	o	4	r	6
	× 3		× 2		× 5		× 5		× 6		× 6

Multiplying magic squares

Each number in this magic square has been multiplied by 2.

Add the rows, columns and diagonals to see if this is a magic square.

8	1	6
3	5	7
4	9	2

×2 →

16	2	12
6	10	14
8	18	4

Make some more magic squares by multiplying each number in the first one by 3, 4, 5 etc.

7	8	
	6	10
9		5

Multiply each number by 3 and fill in the missing numbers to make a new magic square.

Chapter 18: Length 2

Look carefully at a metre stick. It is divided into 100 equal parts.
Each part is called a centimetre.

We can write cm for centimetre or centimetres.

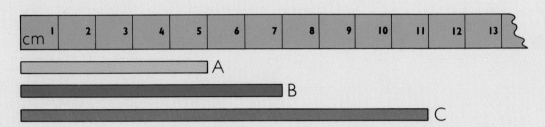

1 How long are the lines A, B and C?
Record like this:

Line A is
☐ cm long.

Line B is
☐ cm long.

Line C is
☐ cm long.

Look at your ruler and see how long it is.

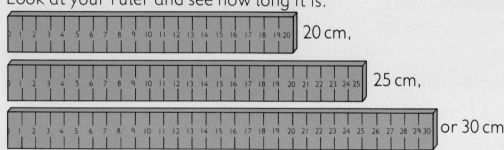

20 cm,

25 cm,

or 30 cm

On some rulers the "0" is right
on the end. This is called
a **dead length** ruler.

When you use this sort of
ruler, the end must be level
with the start of the line.

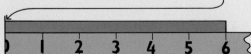

This line is 6 cm long.

On some rulers there is
a **waste end** in case
the corner gets broken off.

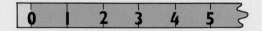

When you use this sort,
the zero mark must be level
with the start of the line.

zero mark

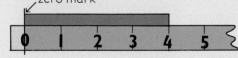

This line is 4 cm long.

When you measure, remember to...

hold your ruler as close to the line as possible,

make sure that the end of the ruler or the zero mark is at the beginning of the line,

hold the ruler firmly as you count the centimetres, I cm, 2 cm. . . .

I Measure the lines carefully.

Record like this:

Line A is ☐ cm long.　　Line B is ☐ cm long.

A

B

C　　　　D

E　　　F

G

Drawing lines the correct length

When you draw lines remember to;

Hold the ruler firmly at the centre.

Start drawing the line from the beginning of the ruler or zero mark.

Check the length of the line is correct before you take your ruler away.

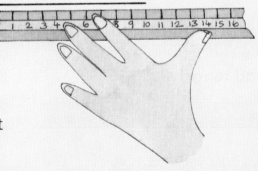

2 Draw these lines:

a 6 cm long	**d** 7 cm long	**g** 4 cm long	**j** 15 cm long
b 12 cm long	**e** 10 cm long	**h** 11 cm long	**k** 13 cm long
c 8 cm long	**f** 2 cm long	**i** 3 cm long	**l** 14 cm long

Measuring distances

·A   ·B

·C

·D

Put the end of
your ruler on the
dot here ➘
✳

1 Record like this:
From ✳ to point **A** is ☐ cm.   From ✳ to point **C** is ☐ cm.

From ✳ to point **B** is ☐ cm.   From ✳ to point **D** is ☐ cm.

2 Estimate the lengths of these lines.
Measure them with a piece of string.
Hold the string taut against the edge
of a ruler to check the measurement.

A
B
C

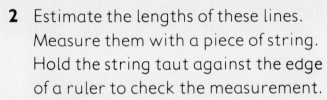
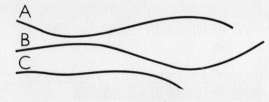

Record like this:

line	estimate	measure
A		
B		
C		

Draw, estimate and measure
some more curved lines.

3 Use a piece of string or tape measure to measure these.
Estimate first. Record like this:

	estimate cm	measurement cm
distance around my neck		
distance around my head		
distance around my waist		
distance round the chalk tin		
distance round a bottle		

Using a metre ruler to measure in centimetres

I Estimate first, then measure these in centimetres.
  a The height of my chair is ☐ cm.
  b The height of my desk is ☐ cm.
  c The width of the door is ☐ cm.
  d The length of my arm is ☐ cm.
  e The height of the radiator is ☐ cm.

Find some more things like these to measure and record.

Using a short ruler to measure longer distances.

If you are careful you can use your own ruler
to measure longer distances.

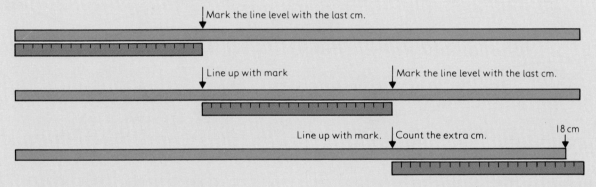

2 Copy the table for your ruler.

20 cm ruler table		25 cm ruler table		30 cm ruler table	
I ruler length	20 cm	I ruler length	25 cm	I ruler length	30 cm
2 ruler lengths	40 cm	2 ruler length	50 cm	2 ruler lengths	60 cm
3 ruler lengths	60 cm	3 ruler lengths	75 cm	3 ruler lengths	90 cm

Record a measurement like this
(Using a 20 cm ruler):

2 ruler lengths and extra part	40 cm
	18 cm
	58 cm

3 Draw some long lines using your metre ruler on a large sheet
of paper. Use your cm ruler to measure the lines.
Record in your book. Check your answers by using a metre ruler.

Addition of centimetres

1 Use your ruler to check your answers to the following.
Record like this. The first is done for you.

a 6 cm + 4 cm = 10 cm. **d** 10 cm + 4 cm = **g** 8 cm + 9 cm =

b 3 cm + 7 cm = **e** 10 cm + 6 cm = **h** 11 cm + 5 cm =

c 5 cm + 5 cm = **f** 10 cm + 8 cm = **i** 7 cm + 11 cm =

2 Measure these strips and record in your book as below.
The first one is done for you.

a

b

c

d

strips	green part		white part		total length
a	7 cm	+	3 cm	=	10 cm

3 Find these measurements on your ruler and work out
the difference between them. The first one is shown here.

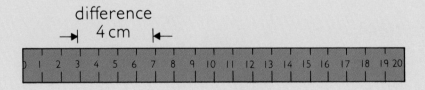

difference
→| 4 cm |←

a 3 cm, 7 cm **c** 5 cm, 15 cm **e** 5 cm, 10 cm **g** 2 cm, 10 cm

b 4 cm, 10 cm **d** 5 cm, 9 cm **f** 6 cm, 16 cm **h** 10 cm, 20 cm

4 Now try these by counting back.

a 9 cm **b** 18 cm **c** 7 cm **d** 19 cm **e** 10 cm **f** 20 cm
  − 6 cm   − 13 cm   − 2 cm   − 11 cm   − 7 cm   − 6 cm

Chapter 19: Introducing fractions 1

This orange is cut into 2 **equal** parts.

Each part is called a **half**.

Half of this flag is black and half is white:

Half of each square is shaded and half is white: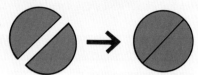

When something is divided into 2 equal parts, each part is called a **half**.
The two **halves** make together 1 whole.

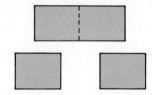

I whole divided into 2 equal parts

$1 \div 2$ is written as $\frac{1}{2}$.

1   Draw some shapes in your book and shade in $\frac{1}{2}$ of each shape.

This cake is cut into 3 **equal** parts.

Each part is called a **third**.

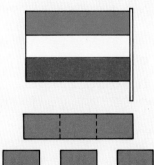

A third of this flag is blue, a third is white and a third is red.

Three **thirds** together make I whole.

I whole divided into 3 equal parts

$1 \div 3$ is written as $\frac{1}{3}$.

2   Draw some shapes in your book.
Divide each shape into 3 **equal** parts. Shade in $\frac{1}{3}$.

I Look at these pictures.

a b c 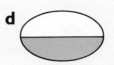 d e f

Write down in your book, in two ways, what part has been shaded?
The first is done for you: **a** half $\frac{1}{2}$.

When I whole is
divided into 4 **equal** parts:
each part is called
a **quarter**
which is written as:

 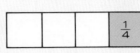

$\frac{1}{4}$ ← I whole
← divided into
← 4 equal parts

4 quarters together
make I whole.

When I whole is
divided into 5 **equal** parts:
each part is called
a **fifth**
which is written as:

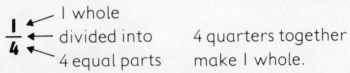

$\frac{1}{5}$ ← I whole
← divided into
← 5 equal parts

Parts of a whole such as
$\frac{1}{2}, \frac{1}{3}, \frac{1}{4}, \frac{1}{5}, \frac{1}{10}$ etc. are called **fractions**.

 The fraction
shaded is $\frac{1}{3}$.

2 Write down the fraction of each shape that is shaded.

a  b c d e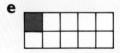

Remember, when I whole is divided into:

2 **equal parts**, each part is called a **half** $\frac{1}{2}$.
3 **equal parts**, each part is called a **third** $\frac{1}{3}$.
4 **equal parts**, each part is called a **quarter** $\frac{1}{4}$.
5 **equal parts**, each part is called a **fifth** $\frac{1}{5}$.
10 **equal parts**, each part is called a **tenth** $\frac{1}{10}$.

We shall look at other fractions later.

This kite shape has been divided into 2 parts but the shaded part is **not** a half because the parts are not **equal**.

Draw another kite in your book and divide it into 2 **equal parts**, that is 2 halves.

I **a** Use a strip of paper.

Fold it into 2 equal parts.

Open it out and colour one half.

Write half on each part.
Paste it into your book.

$\frac{1}{2}$ $\frac{1}{2}$

b Use a strip of paper to show quarters.
Colour the quarters and paste the strip in your book.

2 Here is a strip of centimetre squared paper 10 cm long.

10 cm

5 cm   5 cm

The strip has been divided into 2 equal parts.
This can be written as: $10 \text{ cm} \div 2 = 5 \text{ cm}$ or $\frac{1}{2}$ of $10 \text{ cm} = 5 \text{ cm}$.

Copy and complete two number sentences for each of these pictures:

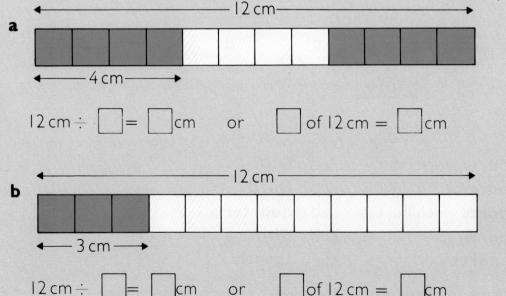

a

12 cm

4 cm

$12 \text{ cm} \div \boxed{} = \boxed{} \text{cm}$ or $\boxed{}$ of $12 \text{ cm} = \boxed{} \text{cm}$

b

12 cm

3 cm

$12 \text{ cm} \div \boxed{} = \boxed{} \text{cm}$ or $\boxed{}$ of $12 \text{ cm} = \boxed{} \text{cm}$

1 The length of this line is 15 cm. It is divided into 3 equal parts.

To find the length of one part we say:
15 cm ÷ 3 = 5 cm or $\frac{1}{3}$ of 15 cm = 5 cm

Write down the two ways of finding the length of a part for:

a 20 cm divided into 2 equal parts

b 8 cm divided into 4 equal parts

c 24 cm divided into 2 equal parts

d 20 cm divided into 10 equal parts

e 16 cm divided into 2 equal parts

f 18 cm divided into 3 equal parts

g 35 cm divided into 5 equal parts

Remember to estimate first.

2 There are 60 minutes in 1 hour. Copy and complete.

a 60 ÷ 2 = ☐   There are ☐ minutes in $\frac{1}{2}$ hour.

b 60 ÷ 4 = ☐   There are ☐ minutes in $\frac{1}{4}$ hour.

c 60 ÷ 3 = ☐   There are ☐ minutes in $\frac{1}{3}$ hour.

3 This bar of chocolate weighs 100 grams.
Copy and complete.

a 100 ÷ 2 = ☐ $\frac{1}{2}$ a bar weighs ☐ grams.

b 100 ÷ 5 = ☐ $\frac{1}{5}$ a bar weighs ☐ grams.

c 100 ÷ 10 = ☐ $\frac{1}{10}$ a bar weighs ☐ grams.

4 There are 24 hours in a day. Copy and complete.

a 24 ÷ 2 = ☐ $\frac{1}{2}$ of a day is ☐ hours.

b 24 ÷ 4 = ☐ $\frac{1}{4}$ of a day is ☐ hours.

c 24 ÷ 3 = ☐ $\frac{1}{3}$ of a day is ☐ hours.

There are 28 dominoes
in a whole set.
They are spread out on
the table face downwards.

To start a game, 4 children divide the whole set of dominoes equally.

$28 \div 4 = 7$ or $\frac{1}{4}$ of $28 = 7$

Each player has a quarter of the dominoes, that is 7 each.

12 chocolates in a box:
$12 \div 3 = 4$ or $\frac{1}{3}$ of $12 = 4$

Ann	Bob	Carol
has	has	has
a third.	a third.	a third.

1 Estimate first. Use counters if you need them.

a $8 \div 2 = \square$ **d** $16 \div 2 = \square$ **g** $\frac{1}{10}$ of $30 = \square$ **j** $12 \div \square = 6$

  $\frac{1}{2}$ of $8 = \square$ $\frac{1}{2}$ of $16 = \square$ $30 \div 10 = \square$ $6 = \square$ of 12

b $15 \div 3 = \square$ **e** $10 \div 5 = \square$ **h** $\frac{1}{4}$ of $16 = \square$ **k** $15 \div \square = 5$

  $\frac{1}{3}$ of $15 = \square$ $\frac{1}{5}$ of $10 = \square$ $16 \div 4 = \square$ $5 = \square$ of 15

c $20 \div 4 = \square$ **f** $24 \div 4 = \square$ **i** $\frac{1}{5}$ of $30 = \square$ **l** $40 \div \square = 4$

  $\frac{1}{4}$ of $20 = \square$ $\frac{1}{4}$ of $24 = \square$ $30 \div 5 = \square$ $10 = \square$ of 40

2 Write down the answers only.

a $\frac{1}{2}$ of 12   **b** $\frac{1}{4}$ of 8   **c** $\frac{1}{3}$ of 6   **d** $\frac{1}{5}$ of 15

  $\frac{1}{4}$ of 16 $\frac{1}{3}$ of 9 $\frac{1}{5}$ of 20 $\frac{1}{2}$ of 16

  $\frac{1}{3}$ of 24 $\frac{1}{2}$ of 40 $\frac{1}{4}$ of 36 $\frac{1}{5}$ of 25

  $\frac{1}{5}$ of 35 $\frac{1}{4}$ of 32 $\frac{1}{2}$ of 14 $\frac{1}{3}$ of 27

Chapter 20: Time 2

Counting hours

An ordinary clock has two hands.
The long hand measures minutes:
The short hand measures hours:

The numbers 1 to 12 show the hours.
The hour hand goes right round
in 12 hours.
There are 24 hours in a day,
so the hour hand goes round
twice a day.

When the minute hand starts at
the top of the clock face, it takes
1 hour (60 minutes) to go round.
During this hour, the small hand
moves from one hour to the next.

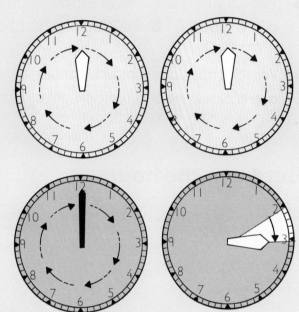

When the minute hand is at the top, the hour hand points exactly
to one of the hour numbers. In the picture it points at 4.
This means that the time is 4 o'clock.

1 Look at these clock faces. Write in your book the times they show:

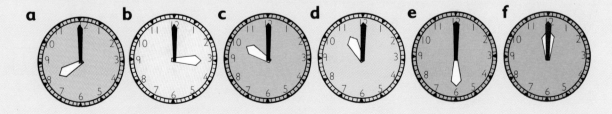

2 Use the clock face rubber stamp to print 4 clock faces
in your book. Draw hands to show these times:

a 7 o'clock   b 1 o'clock   c 5 o'clock   d 9 o'clock

Write the answers to these questions in your book.

1 How many times round the clock does the minute hand go:
  a While the hour hand moves from 12 to 5?
  b While the hour hand goes round once?
  c In one day?

2 How many days does it take the hour hand to go round four times?

3 Which times are 3 hours later than each of these:
  a 1 o'clock   **b** 8 o'clock   **c** 12 o'clock   **d** 10 o'clock

4 Which times are 4 hours earlier than each of these times:
  a 6 o'clock   **b** 4 o'clock   **c** 12 o'clock   **d** 1 o'clock

Between the hours

The minute hand on this clock shows that 10 minutes have passed since 6 o'clock.

One way of writing this time is 6.10. If you have a digital watch, it will show the time like this: `6:10`

Here are some times later in the hour:

The hour hand moves slowly all the time.

6.30 is exactly halfway between the 6 and the 7.

At 6.57 it has almost reached the 7.

Clocks in the 14th century
had an hour hand only
and no minute hand.
You could still tell
roughly what time it was.

1 Write in your book what time this old clock shows.

2 Write down the times these one-handed clocks show.

a 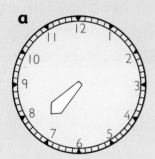 b 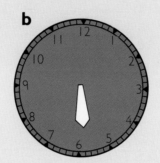 c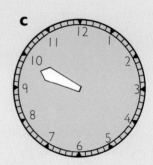

You always write two figures for the minutes.
You write down the time in this way, 6.15, 6.42 and so on.
If the minutes are less than 10, you put a 0 in like this:
6.01, 6.02, 6 o'clock is written 6.00.

3 Look at these clock faces. Write in your book what times they show.

a b c d e f

4 Print clock faces in your book with the rubber stamp.
Draw hands on them in the places where they will be
when a digital watch reads like this:

a `10:15`   c `11:05`   e `11:06`   g `3:33`

b `2:52`   d `7:38`   f `6:30`   h `9:57`

Past and to

At 4.30 the time is exactly halfway between 4 o'clock and 5 o'clock

People say: "It is half past 4."

At 4.15, a quarter ($\frac{1}{4}$) of the time between 4 o'clock and 5 o'clock has passed.

People say: "It is quarter past 4."

At 4.45 three quarters ($\frac{3}{4}$) of the time between 4 o'clock and 5 o'clock has passed. There is a quarter of an hour to go until 5 o'clock so people say "It is quarter to five."

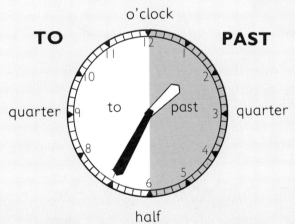

People also say: "10 past 5", "5 past 8", "5 to 7", and so on.

All times after the o'clock and before half past are called **past**.

All times after half past and before the next o'clock are called **to**.

I Look at these clock faces.

Write in your book the times they show.

Write the time both ways for each, for example, "17 minutes past 4" and "4.17" or "23 minutes to 3" and "2.37".

I Write in your book the number of minutes between:

   a 20 past 1 and 20 to 2.   **c** 10 past 7 and 20 to 8.
   b Quarter to 6 and half past 6.   **d** 5 past 6 and 10 past 7.

2 It takes the train 12 minutes to go from Axton to Bigsby.
   If trains leave Axton at 6 o'clock, $\frac{1}{4}$ past 7, 20 to 8 and 9.55,
   at what times would they arrive at Bigsby?

3 Copy this table into your book and try to learn it.

$\frac{1}{2}$ hour is 30 minutes	2 hours are 120 minutes
1 hour is 60 minutes	$2\frac{1}{2}$ hours are 150 minutes
$1\frac{1}{2}$ hours are 90 minutes	3 hours are 180 minutes

4 Write in your book the times which are $1\frac{1}{2}$ hours later than these:

   a 5 o'clock   **c** $\frac{1}{4}$ to 7   **e** 9.05   **g** 3.42
   b $\frac{1}{2}$ past 6   **d** 8.25   **f** 4.33   **h** 7.03

Strange faces

Many clocks and watches
are different.
You may find:

Roman numerals

funny shaped faces

no marks

no numerals

and hands

Here are two very
odd clocks
which are outside
shops in London.
See if you can find
some strange clocks
near where you live.

"What?
R past E
already?"

"It's always about
1 o'clock. Time for lunch
and some fish and chips."

Chapter 21: Division 2

Division and multiplication

These counters have been put into 3 subsets with 5 counters in each. How many counters are there?

Now look at the problem the other way round. Start with 15 counters and put them into 5's. How many subsets?

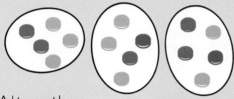

Altogether there are $5 \times 3 = 15$ counters.

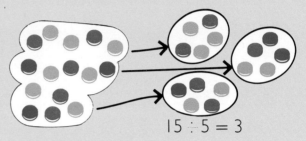

$15 \div 5 = 3$

Division "undoes" what is done by multiplication.

6 in a row, 4 rows
$6 \times 4 = 24$

4 in a column, 6 columns
$4 \times 6 = 24$

24 put in 4 rows, 6 in a row: $24 \div 4 = 6$
24 put in 6 columns, 4 in a column: $24 \div 6 = 4$

1 Use counters or cubes. Put them in columns or rows.
Copy and complete these number sentences.

a $4 \times \square = 12$
$12 \div 4 = \square$
$\square \times 3 = 12$
$12 \div 3 = \square$

c $5 \times \square = 20$
$20 \div 5 = \square$
$\square \times 4 = 20$
$20 \div 4 = \square$

e $6 \times \square = 18$
$18 \div 6 = \square$
$\square \times 3 = 18$
$18 \div 3 = \square$

g $4 \times \square = 16$
$16 \div 4 = \square$

h $5 \times \square = 25$
$25 \div 5 = \square$

b $5 \times \square = 30$
$30 \div 5 = \square$
$\square \times 6 = 30$
$30 \div 6 = \square$

d $9 \times \square = 27$
$27 \div 9 = \square$
$\square \times 3 = 27$
$27 \div 3 = \square$

f $7 \times \square = 28$
$28 \div 7 = \square$
$\square \times 4 = 28$
$28 \div 4 = \square$

i $6 \times \square = 36$
$36 \div 6 = \square$

On the number line:

For multiplication we make equal hops **forwards** →

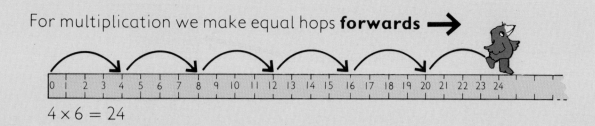

$4 \times 6 = 24$

For division we make equal hops **backwards** ←

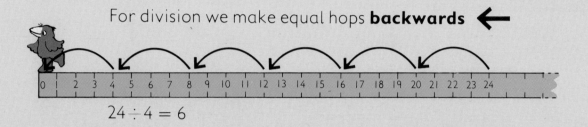

$24 \div 4 = 6$

I Look at these number lines, copy and complete the number sentences.

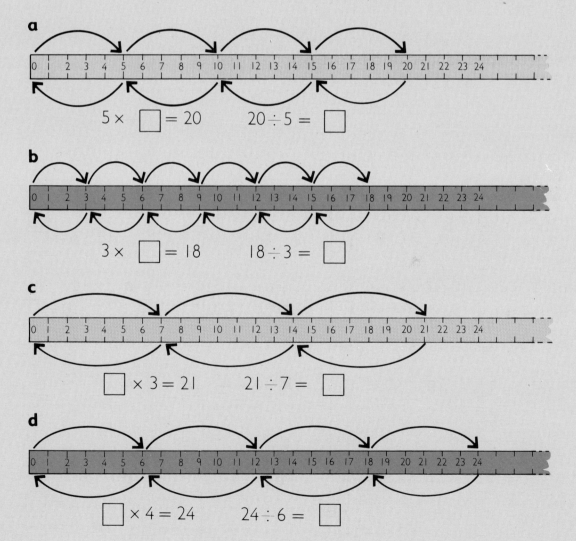

a

$5 \times \boxed{} = 20$ $20 \div 5 = \boxed{}$

b

$3 \times \boxed{} = 18$ $18 \div 3 = \boxed{}$

c

$\boxed{} \times 3 = 21$ $21 \div 7 = \boxed{}$

d

$\boxed{} \times 4 = 24$ $24 \div 6 = \boxed{}$

We can use the multiplication square for division.

6	6	12	18	24	30	36
5	5	10	15	20	25	30
4	4	8	12	16	20	24
3	3	6	9	12	15	18
2	2	4	6	8	10	12
1	1	2	3	4	5	6
×	1	2	3	4	5	6

For $10 \div 5 = \Box$ go along the 5 row until you reach 10.

The 10 is in the 2 column so, $10 \div 5 = \boxed{2}$.

6	6	12	18
5	5	10	15
4	4	8	12
3	3	6	9
2	2	4	6
1	1	2	3
×	1	2	3

1 Copy these into your book and use the square to complete them.

a $6 \div 2 = \Box$ d $12 \div 3 = \Box$ g $8 \div 4 = \Box$ j $20 \div 5 = \Box$

b $4 \div 1 = \Box$ e $20 \div 4 = \Box$ h $18 \div 3 = \Box$ k $15 \div 3 = \Box$

c $10 \div 2 = \Box$ f $5 \div 5 = \Box$ i $24 \div 4 = \Box$ l $30 \div 6 = \Box$

$6 \times 4 = 24$ can be changed into two division sentences.

$24 \div 6 = 4$ and $24 \div 4 = 6$

2 Write the division sentences for:

a $2 \times 6 = 12$
$12 \div 2 = \Box$
$12 \div 6 = \Box$

e $3 \times 8 = 24$
$24 \div 8 = \Box$
$24 \div 3 = \Box$

i $4 \times 7 = 28$
$28 \div 7 = \Box$
$28 \div 4 = \Box$

m $6 \times 3 = 18$
$18 \div 3 = \Box$
$18 \div 6 = \Box$

b $8 \times 4 = 32$
$32 \div 4 = \Box$
$32 \div 8 = \Box$

f $5 \times 4 = 20$
$20 \div 4 = \Box$
$20 \div 5 = \Box$

j $6 \times 4 = 24$
$24 \div 4 = \Box$
$24 \div 6 = \Box$

n $3 \times 10 = 30$
$30 \div 10 = \Box$
$30 \div 3 = \Box$

c $5 \times 3 = 15$
$15 \div 5 = \Box$
$15 \div 3 = \Box$

g $7 \times 5 = 35$
$35 \div 7 = \Box$
$35 \div 5 = \Box$

k $3 \times 4 = 12$
$12 \div 3 = \Box$
$12 \div 4 = \Box$

o $7 \times 2 = 14$
$14 \div 2 = \Box$
$14 \div 7 = \Box$

d $5 \times 6 = 30$
$30 \div 6 = \Box$
$30 \div 5 = \Box$

h $8 \times 3 = 24$
$24 \div 3 = \Box$
$24 : 8 = \Box$

l $7 \times 3 = 21$
$21 \div 3 = \Box$
$21 \div 7 = \Box$

p $6 \times 6 = 36$
$36 \div 6 = \Box$
$36 \div 6 = \Box$

Division with remainders

Try to divide 7 counters or cubes into 3 sub-sets with the same number in each.

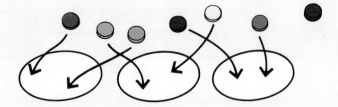

You will have 2 in each sub-set and I left over.

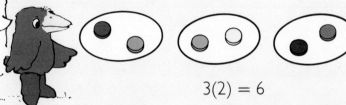

$3(2) = 6$ $\qquad$ $+1$

The one left over is called the **remainder**.

We say:
Seven divided by three is two, remainder one.

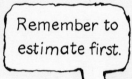

Remember to estimate first.

This is written as:
$7 \div 3 = 2$, remainder 1.

1 Now take 14 counters or cubes and divide them into 4 equal sub-sets. Draw a picture of your answer in your book, copy and complete the number sentence.

$14 \div 4 = \Box$, remainder $\triangle$

2 Use counters or cubes for these:

a $9 \div 2 = \Box$, remainder $\triangle$ $\qquad$ e $11 \div 4 = \Box$, remainder $\triangle$

b $17 \div 5 = \Box$, remainder $\triangle$ $\qquad$ f $10 \div 3 = \Box$, remainder $\triangle$

c $20 \div 6 = \Box$, remainder $\triangle$ $\qquad$ g $23 \div 4 = \Box$, remainder $\triangle$

d $17 \div 8 = \Box$, remainder $\triangle$ $\qquad$ h $33 \div 6 = \Box$, remainder $\triangle$

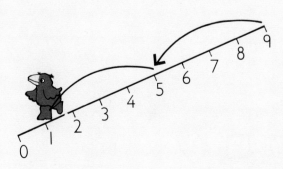

Remainders can be shown on a number line.
Divide 9 into sub-sets with 4 in each.
It takes 2 hops to reach 1. There are not enough for another hop so 1 is left over.

$9 \div 4 = 2$, remainder 1.

1 Look at these number lines. Copy and complete the number sentences.

a

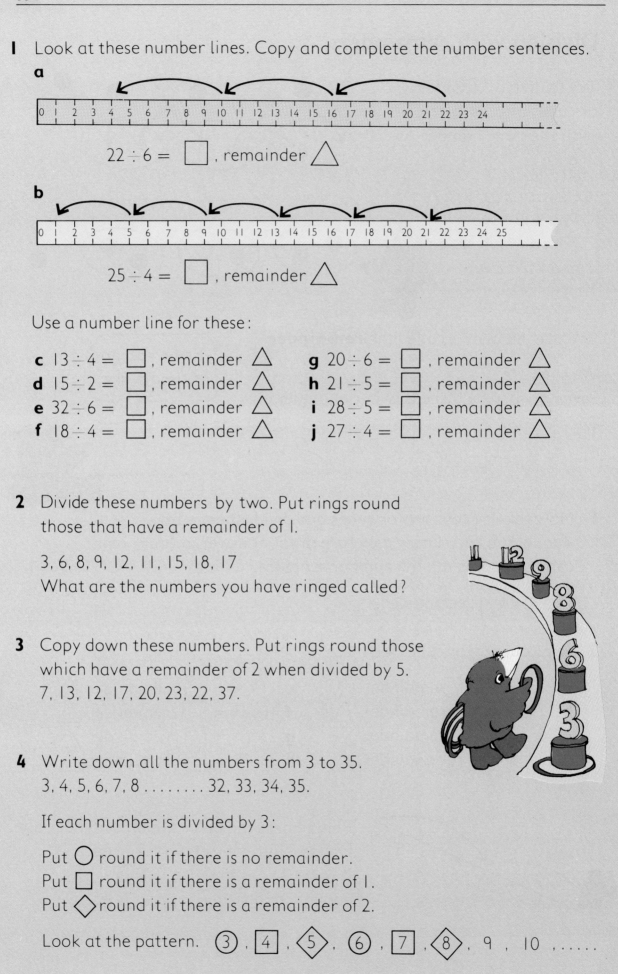

0 1 2 3 4 5 6 7 8 9 10 11 12 13 14 15 16 17 18 19 20 21 22 23 24

$22 \div 6 = \square$, remainder $\triangle$

b

0 1 2 3 4 5 6 7 8 9 10 11 12 13 14 15 16 17 18 19 20 21 22 23 24 25

$25 \div 4 = \square$, remainder $\triangle$

Use a number line for these:

c $13 \div 4 = \square$, remainder $\triangle$ g $20 \div 6 = \square$, remainder $\triangle$

d $15 \div 2 = \square$, remainder $\triangle$ h $21 \div 5 = \square$, remainder $\triangle$

e $32 \div 6 = \square$, remainder $\triangle$ i $28 \div 5 = \square$, remainder $\triangle$

f $18 \div 4 = \square$, remainder $\triangle$ j $27 \div 4 = \square$, remainder $\triangle$

2 Divide these numbers by two. Put rings round those that have a remainder of 1.

3, 6, 8, 9, 12, 11, 15, 18, 17
What are the numbers you have ringed called?

3 Copy down these numbers. Put rings round those which have a remainder of 2 when divided by 5.
7, 13, 12, 17, 20, 23, 22, 37.

4 Write down all the numbers from 3 to 35.
3, 4, 5, 6, 7, 8 . . . . 32, 33, 34, 35.

If each number is divided by 3:

Put ◯ round it if there is no remainder.
Put ☐ round it if there is a remainder of 1.
Put ◇ round it if there is a remainder of 2.

Look at the pattern. ③ , ④ , ⬥5⬥ , ⑥ , ⑦ , ⬥8⬥ , 9 , 10 , ...

Chapter 22: Weight 2

The handy "hecto"

Four apples weigh much less
than 1 kg and much more than 1 g.
These weights are not a handy size.

People in Italy use
an inbetween weight of 100 g.
The weight's real name is "hectogram".
The Italians call it "etto" for short.
We will call it "hecto".

1 Pick up a "hecto" weight. Get the feel of it.
    a Estimate how many marbles weigh 1 hecto (100 g). Then estimate
       how many pencils, crayons, sweets, rulers, pebbles weigh 100 g.

    b Use a balance and a hecto weight to see how close your estimates are.
       Record in your book :
       ☐ marbles balance 1 hecto (100 g), and so on.
       ☐ marbles ☐ pencils ☐ crayons ☐ sweets ☐ rulers ☐ pebbles

2 Take a piece of modelling clay and roll it into a ball
    that you think will weigh 100 g.
    Check with your hecto weight on the balance.
    Add or take away some clay till it balances.

3 Use an eggcup as a measure for
    rice, dried peas, sand and sawdust.
    Find how many eggcupfuls of each
    weigh a hecto. Record like this :
    ☐ eggcupfuls of rice balance 1 hecto.

    a eggcupfuls of rice   **b** eggcupfuls of sand   **c** eggcupfuls of sawdust

The hecto and the kilogram

Your family bakes you a birthday cake.

It weighs I kg.

Altogether there are 10 people at your party so you cut the cake into 10 equal slices.

Each slice is a tenth of the whole cake.

I hecto is	100 g	
2 hectos are	200 g	
3 hectos are	300 g	
4 hectos are	400 g	
5 hectos are	500 g	← (half a kg)
6 hectos are	600 g	
7 hectos are	700 g	
8 hectos are	800 g	
9 hectos are	900 g	
10 hectos are	1000 g	← (I kg)

I a How much does each slice weigh?
b Can you count in hundreds?
Copy the table into your book so that you can remember it.

Using hecto weights

Use hecto weights on the balance to weigh:

400 grams of pebbles   300 grams of sand   500 grams of
900 grams of potatoes   200 grams of bottle tops   modelling clay.

Here is a recipe for 12 small cakes:

2 eggs
I hecto (100 g) margarine
I hecto (100 g) sugar
I hecto (100 g) flour

Cream the margarine and sugar together in a bowl.
Add the 2 eggs and beat together in a bowl.
Add the flour and a little milk to make a creamy mixture.
Put in small cake tins and bake for 15 minutes until golden in a moderately hot oven (Gas No. 5 electricity 300).

I Find at least 20 different objects.
Pick each one up and estimate what it weighs.
Now use the balance and hecto weights to check your estimate.

Make a chart like this to record.
Remember – always estimate before weighing.

weight	object	
	estimate	using balance
less than 100 g	rubber, pencil	rubber, pencil
100 to 200 g		
200 to 300 g	maths book	
300 to 400 g		maths book
400 to 500 g		
500 to 600 g		
700 to 800 g		
800 to 900 g		
900 to 1 kg		
over 1 kg		

In this example, the weight of the maths book was
estimated as more than 2 hectos but less than 3 hectos,
that is, between 200 g and 300 g.
On the balance, it weighed between 300 g and 400 g.

Weighing people

We use kilograms
to weigh people.

A grown-up man usually
weighs about 80 or 90 kg.

A new-born baby
usually weighs about 3 kg.

Make a graph like this on squared paper showing your weight and the weights of some of your friends.

Using smaller weights

Earlier you weighed some things that were less than 100 g.
Now you will be able to find what they really weigh, using these smaller weights on the balance.

1 Copy this table into your book and complete it:

30 g	20 g + 10 g
40 g	
60 g	
80 g	
50 g	
90 g	
70 g	

2 Copy these into your book and use the balance and weights to help you complete them:

a ☐ marbles weigh 70 g.

b ☐ sweets weight 60 g

c ☐ bottle tops weigh 50 g

d ☐ pencils weigh 40 g

e ☐ 50 g weights weigh 100 g

f ☐ 10 g weights weigh 100 g

g ☐ 10 g weights weigh 50 g

h ☐ 20 g weights weigh 100 g.

Chapter 23: Area

Which is larger?
The surface
A or B?

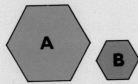

When the surfaces
are the same shape it
is easy to compare them by placing one
on the other to see which is the larger.

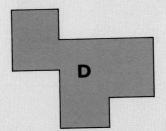

What about these?
Which is the larger,
C or D?

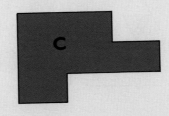

To find out which surface
is the larger we must
compare their **areas**.
Area is the amount of surface.
The two surfaces can be
covered with match boxes
like this:

1 **a** How many match boxes does it take to cover shape C?
 b How many match boxes does it take to cover shape D?
 c Which shape has the greater area?

2 **a** Estimate the number of exercise books you would need to
 cover the top of your desk, remember the books must not overlap.
 b Fit the exercise books on the top of the desk to cover it.
 How many did you use? How close was your estimate?

3 Take a pack of playing cards.
 Estimate first and then by covering the surfaces,
 count how many cards are needed to cover the surface of:
 a an exercise book **b** this maths book **c** the seat of your chair

Which shapes cover best?

Some shapes are better than others for covering surfaces:

These fit together and do not leave spaces.

These do not fit together – there are spaces between them.

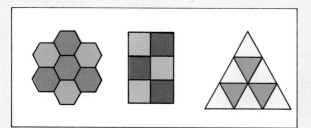 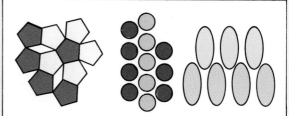

Area

These shapes have the same area because each needs 8 triangles of the same size to cover it.

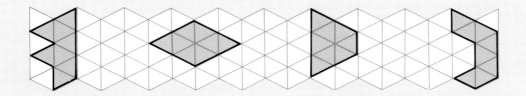

We could write, "Each shape has an area of 8 units."

I By counting the units, compare the area of each shape with its partner. The first one is done for you.
Shape A has an area of 13 units. Shape B has an area of 9 units.
The area of shape A is greater than the area of Shape B.

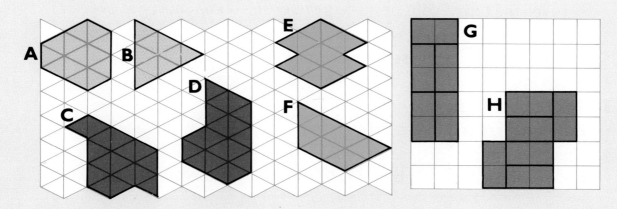

Area by counting squares

The tiles on bathroom walls or lino tiles on the floor
are usually square. It is easier to cover most surfaces
with squares than with any other shape.

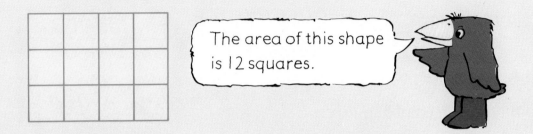

The area of this shape
is 12 squares.

1 In your book write the area of the following surfaces.
   The first one is done for you. **A** The area is 9 squares.

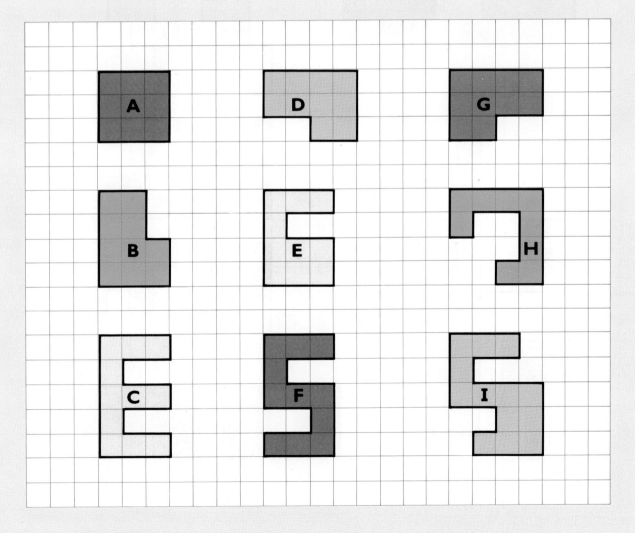

1 On squared paper draw:

    a 3 different shapes, each with an area of 10 squares.

    b 3 different shapes, each with an area of 18 squares.

2 In your book write down the area of each shape by counting the squares and then compare it with its partner.
The first is done for you.

Shape **A** has an area of 9 squares.

Shape **B** has an area of 8 squares.

Shape **A** has a greater area than shape **B**.

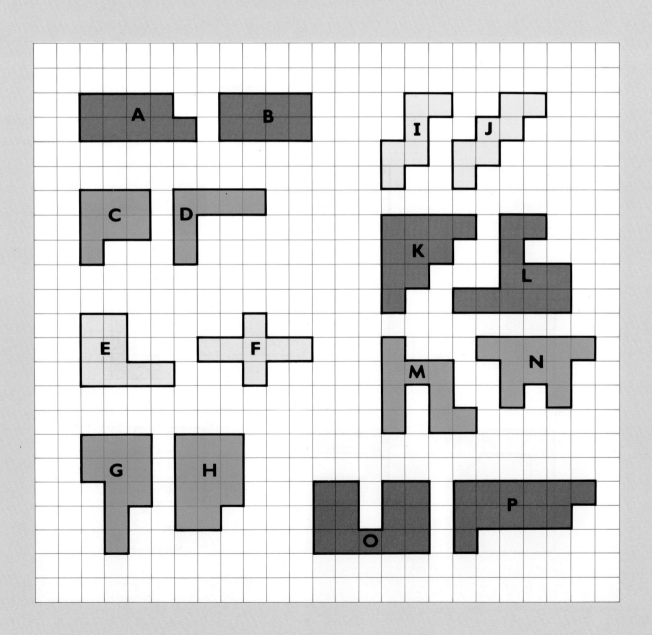

Chapter 24: Capacity 2 and volume

Standard measures of capacity

1 Make a list of as many liquids
as you can.

Make a collection of
empty containers in which
different liquids have been sold.

2 Look carefully at the labels to
see if the amount is recorded
in litres or millilitres —
ml may be used for millilitres.
Make a list of these amounts
in your book like this:

container for	capacity
paint	
vinegar	
wine	
orange squash	
bitter lemon	

Liquids are sold in standard amounts
(litres or parts of a litre) so that
people know how much they are buying.

3 Look at a 1 litre measure.
Could you drink a litre
of water in one go?

4 Take a drinking glass and
find how many times you
can fill it from 1 litre.

Some containers are larger than 1 litre

5 How many litres fill a bucket?

The half litre (500 ml)

The small measure here
holds 500 millilitres
(500 ml for short).

1 How many times can
you fill the 500 ml measure
from 1 litre of water?

2 Take 10 containers and label them with the letters of
the alphabet A, B, C, and so on up to J.

Copy this table into your book. Find out what each container holds.
Put a tick in the right box to complete your table.

container	holds less than 500 ml	holds 500 ml to 1 litre	holds more than 1 litre
A			
B			
C			
D			
E			
F			
G			
H			
I			
J			

3 Make a collection of bottles which hold half a litre or more.
Fill each one with 500 ml of water. Mark the water level on
the side with a wax crayon. Do some of the levels surprise you?

Cuboids, volume and cubes

These containers are taking up space on a shelf.

Some shapes pack together without spaces between them.
The space that something takes up is called its **volume**.

The boxes on the left take up about the same volume as the odd shaped containers on the right, but the boxes pack together better.

Cubes and cuboids pack together much better than spheres, cylinders or cones.

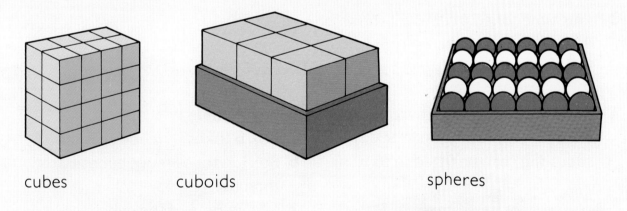

cubes   cuboids   spheres

cylinders   cones

Fitting cubes together

Here are two walls made
out of cubes.

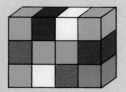

1 a How many cubes are there in each of the walls?
   b Do the two walls have the same volume?

2 Take 12 cubes all the same size.
Arrange them to make as many cuboids as you can.
Record your cuboids in a table like this in your book.

	number of layers	number of cubes in each layer	number of cubes used
cuboid 1			12
cuboid 2			12

and so on . . . .
Stack cubes together to measure the volume of a space.
Find the volume by counting the number of cubes in each layer,
and the number of layers, then multiply the numbers together.

3 This time take 24 cubes all the same size.
Arrange them to make as many cuboids as you can.
Record your cuboids in a table as you did before.

4 Here are two boxes. In front of
each box is the biggest stack of
cubes that can be fitted in to it.

a Box A takes ☐ cubes
   Box B takes ☐ cubes
b Box ☐ takes more cubes
   than box ☐
c The volume of the cubes
   in ☐ is greater than the
   volume of the cubes in ☐

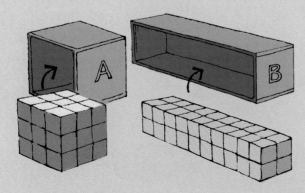

5 Collect or make more boxes and find out how many cubes they hold.

Chapter 25: Probability

Getting to know dice

How are the spots arranged on a 'correct' die?

If you use a mirror you will see that the number of spots on the opposite sides of a 'correct' die add up to seven.

1

Which of these is not a 'correct' die?
Draw the three 'correct' dice and under each write the numbers you cannot see.

2

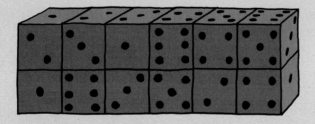

How many spots are there on the back of this wall?

3 Make a 'correct' die from a blank cube and some spots.
How many spots will you need?

4 Use eight 'correct' dice to make a cube.
What is the smallest number of spots you can have showing on the outside of the cube?
What is the largest number of spots you can have showing?

1 Drawing a cat

Play with a friend.
Take it in turns to roll a die.
To draw the cat, each player must
throw these scores in order.

Throw a 1 to draw the face.
Throw a 2 to draw the body.
Throw a 3 to draw the ears.
Throw a 4 to draw the eyes.
Throw a 5 to draw the tail.
Throw a 6 to draw the whiskers.

The first player to draw a complete cat
wins the game.
Play the game six times. Keep a record of how many times
you win and how many times your friend wins.
Do you think the game is fair? That is, do you and your
friend have an equal chance of winning? Give a reason.

2 Odd and even

Play with a friend.
Start with nine counters each.
One player chooses the odd numbers,
the other player chooses the even numbers.
Take it in turns to roll a die. Whatever number you score,
take that number of counters from your friend.
For example, if you have chosen the odd numbers and you
roll a take 3 counters from your friend's pile of counters.

But if you roll ⚁ or ⚃ or ⚅ , you cannot take any
counters because you have chosen the odd numbers.
Play until one player wins by gaining all 18 counters.
Play the game five times and record how many times 'odd' wins
and how many times 'even' wins.
Is this game fair? Do both players have an equal chance of
winning?
How can you make the game fair?

Logibloc games

I This is a game for four players.
You will need a four-sided shapes spinner, a set of *Logiblocs* and a score chart.

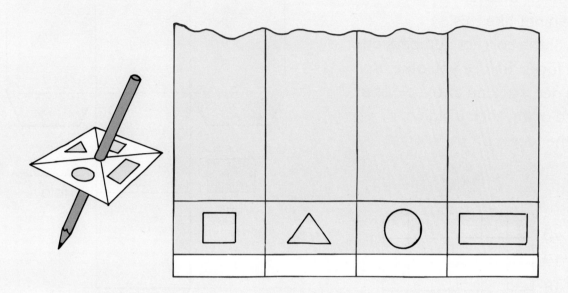

Each player chooses a shape and writes his or her name under that shape on the score sheet.
Take it in turns to spin the spinner.
If it lands on your shape, place a matching block on the score chart.
The first player to use up all the blocks of one shape wins.
Is the game fair? Give your reasons.
Play the game eight times.
Did everyone win the same number of times?
Do you still think the game is fair? Give your reasons.

2 This is another game for four players.
You will need a set of *Logiblocs*, a score chart as in the first game but this time you will need a six-sided spinner like this.

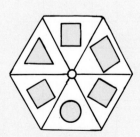

Each player chooses a shape and the game is played as before.
Is this game fair?
Which shape is most likely to run out first?

Biased dice

Most dice are fair.
Rolling 1, 2, 3, 4, 5 or 6 is
equally likely.
You can make a die that is
unfair or biased.
Use a net like this.
Mark the correct numbers on
the faces. Before you glue up
the net, stick an extra piece of
card or Blutack inside one
of the faces.

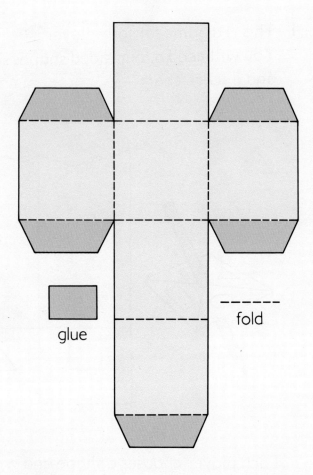

glue   fold

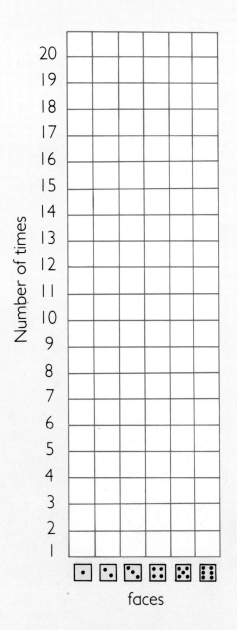

See if your friend can discover
what the bias of your die is.

Draw a graph like this on
squared paper.
Roll the biased die 20 times.
Colour in a square for each
number rolled.

Does the graph show you the bias
of your die—that is the number
more likely to be rolled?